SHORT
NATURE
WALKS
IN CONNECTICUT

"The definitive guide on the subject of nature walks and hiking in the Nutmeg State. Chock-full of maps, advice, and historical tidbits."

—*Danbury News-Times*

"For most, a single day or just a few hours can be adequate for the short journey to 'get away from it all.' Complete information on trails and other hiking areas throughout the state."

—*The Day* (New London)

"A most appropriate book for nature lovers to aid them in their explorations. . . . This book is a compact guide that helps the reader discover the treasures of nature. . . . Especially for those people who live in Connecticut, this book is a treasure."

—*The Litchfield County Times*

"[This guide] lets the urban hermit in on options for walks in the Connecticut countryside."

—*The Advocate* newspapers

"A guide to escaping to the woods, forests, mountains, lakes, and beaches of Connecticut's Blue Trails system. Using this compact guide, you and your family can enjoy a few hours in the woods any season of the year and leave civilization behind."

etter

Help Us Keep This Guide Up to Date

Every effort has been made by the author and editors to make this guide as accurate and useful as possible. However, many things can change after a guide is published—establishments close, phone numbers change, hiking trails are rerouted, facilities come under new management, and so on.

We would love to hear from you concerning your experiences with this guide and how you feel it could be made better and be kept up to date. While we may not be able to respond to all comments and suggestions, we'll take them to heart and we'll also make certain to share them with the author. Please send your comments and suggestions to the following address:

The Globe Pequot Press
Reader Response/Editorial Department
P.O. Box 833
Old Saybrook, CT 06475

Or you may e-mail us at:

editorial@globe-pequot.com

Thanks for your input, and happy travels!

SHORT NATURE WALKS
IN CONNECTICUT

Sixth Edition

by EUGENE KEYARTS

revised by CHRIS BRUNSON

The
Globe
Pequot
Press

OLD SAYBROOK, CONNECTICUT

Copyright © 1979 by Eugene Keyarts
Revised material copyright © 1988, 1991, 1994, 1997, 1999 by The Globe
Pequot Press

Cover design: Saralyn D'Amato-Twomey
Cover photograph: McConnell/McNamara

Library of Congress Cataloging-in-Publication Data
Keyarts, Eugene.
    Short nature walks in Connecticut / by Eugene Keyarts. — 6th ed. /
revised by Chris Brunson.
       p. cm. — (Short nature walks series)
    ISBN 0-7627-0439-X
    1. Hiking—Connecticut Guidebooks. 2. Natural history—Connecticut
Guidebooks. 3. Connecticut Guidebooks. I. Brunson, Chris. II. Title.
III. Series.
GV199.42.C8K5 1999
917.4604'43—dc21   99-22421
                                                            CIP

Manufactured in the United States of America
Sixth Edition/First Printing

To Jesse Brunson—
for all your work.

Contents

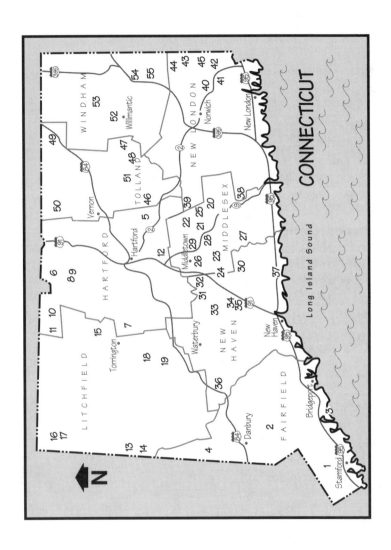

Middlesex County

New Haven County

New London County

Tolland County

Windham County

Introduction

Connecticut's diverse landscape encompasses one-of-a-kind natural features: traprock ridges, the remnants of a volcanic past, and evidence of glaciation when the Ice Age locked up New England and rumbled across Connecticut, leaving behind massive boulders. Waterfalls, gorges, ponds, streams, and ocean are all natural features of a varied terrain.

The cultural past is in evidence as well—from the history of Native Americans who traveled trails now named for tribes (some of whom have made their home in the state for 10,000 years) to the everyday farmers and folks who fought for American independence or during the Civil War. Mute testimony to the state's past can be seen while out on a walk—old stone walls, ruins of old mills, abandoned mines and quarries. The varied microclimates created by natural features create homes for a bewildering amount of plant and animal life—from exquisite orchids and blueberry bushes to bobcat and chipmunks—all within the boundaries of a quite compact state.

In September thousands of hawks migrate along the invisible sky highway south through the state; in late winter the American bald eagle calls the banks of the Connecticut River home and fishes its waters.

If you think that open space and natural areas are not available because of our state's dense population, then you are in for a pleasant surprise. Connecticut is second to none in what it has to offer a hiker or walker.

The Connecticut Forest and Park Association maintains more than 700 miles of cleared and well-marked woodland trails throughout the state; many of the walks in this book are on these trails. They are known as the Connecticut Blue Trail System because they are marked with blue "blazes" of paint on trees and rocks, and they touch every county of the state. Many state parks have hiking trails, as do numerous areas looked after by local land trusts and other groups. Connecticut's Department of Environmental Protection aims to identify and increase open space, and the southeastern portion of the state sponsors an annual walk day extravaganza. Recently the Connecticut River was named an American Heritage River, and towns along its banks are working on access and trails to the water.

From your home you can reach even the most distant of these trails within a few hours, have plenty of time to explore the trail, spend a picnic hour in pleasant surroundings, sometimes learn a bit of history, and then return home at a leisurely pace that night.

Who hasn't wished to escape, if only for a few hours, the pressures of modern living? Who hasn't wanted to get away from the hustle and hurry, away from the crowd, to go on foot into the woods and fields?

Short Nature Walks in Connecticut will inform those nature lovers just where they may pursue their interests freely without the restrictions of NO TRESPASSING signs. Whether you are interested in wildflowers, rocks, minerals, birds, trees, history—or just a walk—you will find what you are looking for in abundance along the trail.

This guide contains fifty-five short walks. The walks are compiled according to county. The maps for each walk are not according to scale, but are intended to show the relationship of the trail to roads and other landmarks and to clarify the written directions.

The more than 700 miles of the Connecticut Blue Trail System—and the other trails in this book—are not for the sole use of hiking clubs or the dyed-in-the-wool hiker. These trails offer opportunity to not only explore and discover woods and waters, but a chance to escape the hustle and bustle and to make lasting memories.

—*Chris Brunson*

What to Wear and Bring

The equipment required for these short walks in Connecticut need not be elaborate. However good footwear is a must. Wear sturdy shoes, preferably boots that support and protect ankles with a cleated composition sole. (Leather soles are apt to become slippery.) Don't break in a pair of new footwear on a walk—your feet will be grateful. Equip children with good shoes or boots as well; their comfort will make your walk more enjoyable.

Two pairs of socks will cushion the feet and also absorb excessive perspiration. If you cannot tolerate wool against your skin, wear a pair of light cotton or silk socks underneath a pair of wool socks.

Items that may prove helpful include insect repellent, tissues, a basic first-aid kit, and sunglasses. A light knapsack in which to carry these items, as well as lunch and other gear, is especially useful as it leaves the hands free.

Wear comfortable clothing: Loose-fitting pants are better than shorts; a lightweight sweater or flannel shirt gives extra warmth; a windbreaker or parka provides protection against wind and rain. A wide-brimmed hat has several advantages: It protects the eyes from glaring sun; it keeps rain or snow off neck and face; and it gives slightly more protection from insects.

It's advisable to carry water wherever you walk. A thermos filled with hot or cold liquid is a nice trail treat. Take a suitable lunch, depending on how much time you plan to spend on the trail. Food may vary from sandwiches to fruit and raisins. There's nothing quite like fresh air to whet an appetite and add flavor to a simple meal.

You may want to bring along binoculars or a camera, but be careful not to overload yourself with too much gear. A map and compass may not be absolutely essential but are recommended—as is a detailed topographical map. Sometimes a good way to get familiar with a trail is to go on a guided hike first. Losing your way is not funny and can be dangerous if you get hurt or the weather turns severe. Also, never start a walk at dusk.

Take along a field guide to flowers, trees, birds, rocks, or other subjects, depending on your particular interests. These can add to the enjoyment and educational value of any walk.

SPECIAL NOTE: BEFORE YOU WALK

Change is the rule of nature; but her changes are slow, barely perceptible, and usually beneficial. Humans, in contrast, make drastic changes to solve immediate problems, only to create more harmful situations for the future.

Because of man-made changes—superhighways, crowded developments, and shopping complexes—we continue to destroy acres and acres of irreplaceable natural areas.

Since disruption and change is inevitable, we can only suggest that the user of this guide accept and comply with all trespass regulations. In many instances, however, a polite request of the property owner for permission to follow a trail over private land is usually granted. And in every instance, the rule to remember is "Take only pictures; leave only footprints."

Beware of Hunters

If you live in a suburban area, hunting is something you may not even be aware of; however, throughout much of the state, hunting is a regular activity, especially in autumn. Don't assume where you hike is off-limits. If you are alert and use your common sense, you can still take pleasant walks during this season, but be sure to wear bright (blaze orange is best) clothing.

Walkers should be aware that peak hunting season for small game and deer falls between the third Saturday in October through December, especially in the early morning hours. No Sunday hunting is allowed in the state, except at registered private shooting preserves. Hunting does not occur in most state parks and incidents involving non-hunters are extremely rare.

Caution. . .

When walking in the woods, grassland, or marshland, take precautions against ticks, especially the deer tick, *Ixodes dammini.* The bite of some ticks transmits a spirochete bacterium, which may cause Lyme disease. (Early symptoms of Lyme disease are a rash or red patch on the skin, muscle ache, fever, chills, and fatigue.)

To prevent tick bites, wear your shirt tucked into long pants with pant cuffs tucked into socks. White or light-colored clothing makes it easier to spot ticks. Insect repellents may be useful. Brush off clothing and pets when you return home. Undress and check for ticks: They usually crawl about for several hours before burrowing into your skin. Be vigilant—check leg and arm creases and heads and necks especially thoroughly.

Remove any ticks you find with tweezers (saving the tick in a jar for future reference); then wash the area and your hands with soap and water. If you develop symptoms of Lyme disease, consult a physician immediately.

Also be aware that over the years rattlesnakes have occasionally been reported in some areas, particularly in the Meshomasic Forest and near rock exposures and traprock cliffs. Use common sense: Snakes like to bask in the sun's warmth—often on the same rock cliffs you want to walk across. Hikers should always wear sturdy shoes (those that protect ankles) and be alert to their surroundings.

You should also use precautions, especially when walking in southeastern Connecticut during the summer, against mosquitoes. In recent years a few mosquitoes in this area have been found to carry a rare but serious disease called Eastern Equine Encephalitis (EEE). Fortunately there has never been a documented human case of EEE in the state, but in 1990 four horses died from the disease.

To protect yourself from mosquito bites you should avoid walking when the mosquitoes are most active—at dawn and at dusk—or wear long-sleeved shirts and long pants. Also use a mosquito repellent that contains DEET and follow the directions on the label.

It's always a good idea to leave word at home or some other place regarding your plans. And one should never walk alone. Sharing with family and friends the pleasures of natural beauty and healthful activity will prove rewarding.

Lastly, don't overdo it while out walking; remember to turn back *before* tiring.

Trail Information

After you have walked some or all the trails listed in *Short Nature Walks in Connecticut* you may want some additional information about Connecticut trails.

For information about the Connecticut Blue Trails, write to:

Connecticut Forest and Park Association
16 Meriden Road
Rockfall, CT 06481
Web site: www.ctwoodlands.org

For other information about state trails, nature centers, state parks, greenways, forests, and natural history, write to:

State of Connecticut Department of Environmental Protection
Parks, Forests and State Lands
79 Elm Street
Hartford, CT 06106
Web site: www.dep.state.ct.us

Appalachian Trail Conference
P.O. Box 807
Harpers Ferry, WV 25425
Web site: www.atconf.org

Appalachian Mountain Club
5 Joy Street
Boston, MA 02108
(617) 523–0636
Web site: www.outdoors.org

Adirondack Mountain Club
814 Goggins Road
Lake George, NY 12845
(800) 395–8080
Web site: www.adk.org

Adirondack Mountain Club Connecticut Valley Chapter
c/o Arthur Potwin
128 Shingle Mill Road
Harwinton, CT 06791

For topographic maps to supplement
trail maps in this book, write:

U.S. Geological Survey
Washington, DC 20242

State topographical maps and publications about geology, botany, and more are available from the Department of Environmental Protection store located at 79 Elm Street, Hartford, Connecticut.

For information about an annual walking weekend in the Quinebaug and Shetucket Rivers Valley National Heritage Corridor (northeast Connecticut), write: Walking Weekend, Northeast Connecticut Visitors District, P.O. Box 598, Putnam, CT 06260. Walks encompass tours for every age and fitness level; they include natural history, bird watching, and the arts.

There are thousands of miles of walking trails throughout every state in the nation. You will find them in all national parks and in many state forests and state parks. For information write to the Conservation Department in the state you are interested in.

Bartlett Arboretum

Stamford

A living showcase of trees, shrubs, plants, and flowers with many different walk options, including a swamp boardwalk. There is something here for everyone to enjoy.

Walkers of all ages and abilities can discover a branch of the natural world at the Bartlett Arboretum of the University of Connecticut at Stamford.

An arboretum is a living museum of plants growing under a variety of conditions. The Bartlett Arboretum offers opportunities to explore living bamboo, a collection of "witches' broom" trees, a secluded garden, a collection of nut trees, and a swamp walk—all in addition to educational programs for the public and professionals in horticulture and plant science. A variety of workshops and occasional plant sales are offered as well.

> **TRAIL TIPS**
>
> A large map board is located in a gazebo near the parking lot; portable rest rooms are in the same area.

The Bartlett Arboretum is open to the general public, free of charge. (Donations are welcome.) Take a convenient route to the intersection of Merritt Parkway exit 35 and Route 137 (High Ridge Road). From the intersection, drive north on Route 137 for 1.4 miles to Brookdale Road.

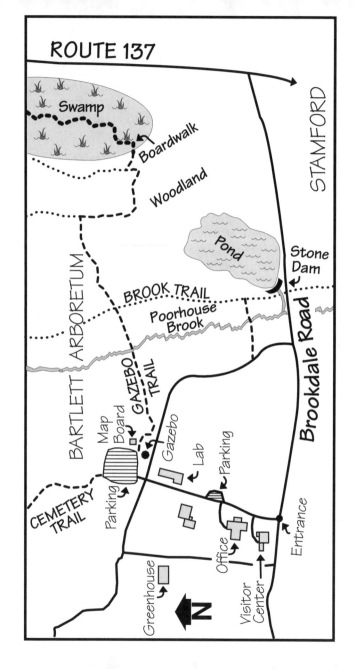

Turn west onto Brookdale Road and follow it to a road on the right, which is the well-marked entrance drive to the arboretum. Follow signs to the parking area. At the office, obtain a free map and brochure from the personnel in charge, who will also answer your questions. A backpack filled with children's activities and games to use on a visit may be checked out here; return it when you leave. A small, but well-stocked shop offers neat things: compasses (under $4.00), books, notecards, gardener's soap, and related items.

There are trails, not blazed but well defined, that crisscross the mixed-hardwood forest, a red maple swamp, Poorhouse Stream, and a 2-acre pond on the 50-acre woodland and swamp areas. One may observe and study the trees, wildlife, and wildflowers. An interesting feature is a sturdy boardwalk winding through the swamp and bog areas—fun in springtime when turtles and frogs are abundant. A perennial garden is sure to inspire any gardener seeking fresh ideas.

In 1913 Dr. Francis Bartlett, a dendrologist (an expert in trees and plants) and founder of the Bartlett Tree Ex-

TELLING THE SEASON BY PLANTS AND SOUNDS

If any season may be considered superior, it has to be spring. The poet Henry Van Dyke wrote, "The first day of spring is one thing, and the first spring day is another. The difference between them is sometimes as great as a month."

Whether spring is on time or comes a bit late, it is a period of anticipation and fascination. The skunk cabbage pushes up a tentative probe but is careful to keep her cowled hood tightly closed. The red-winged blackbird suddenly announces his arrival, sounding his cheery unmistakable *ok-a-lee* call while clinging to a swaying upright reed. When the bloodroot and shadbush flaunt their white blossoms and the yellow adder's-tongue cautiously appears, spring is truly here.

pert Company, acquired the farm as his home and established a school and laboratory for his company. Through the years he assembled a large number of plant specimens from around the world. In 1965 the research lab was moved to North Carolina and the North Stamford property was bought by the state of Connecticut.

The arboretum staff and members of the Bartlett Arboretum Association are constantly working on and offering varied programs of interest to the novice and expert alike. Tours are conducted by appointment. It is requested that appointments be made at least one week in advance. For information, contact: The Bartlett Arboretum, 151 Brookdale Road, Stamford 06903; (203) 322–6971.

IN THE AREA

The Stamford Nature Center is located nearby. Stamford also has a wealth of places for eating out and trail supplies.

It is not necessary to take a guided tour. To the student of nature there is something of interest taking place at all times and in every season at the arboretum. The Rose A. Thielens Self-Guided Ecology Walk corresponds to numbered stations along the walks. The booklet is available at the office for $1.00.

Putnam Memorial
Redding

A walk through a pristine park with historic ruins. All abilities can enjoy this walk, which includes exploring a museum and a cave.

Connecticut has its own Valley Forge—one most residents aren't even aware exists.

The Putnam Memorial State Park in Redding, Connecticut, memorializes the site of the winter encampment of the right wing of the Continental Army during the winter of 1778 to 1779. This walk is not so much on leaf-strewn trails as it is a meander through the leaves of American history.

The historic park comprises more than 230 acres and includes one of the best preserved winter campsites of the Revolutionary War. In this area between 8,000 to 9,000 troops suffered through that stormy winter. General Washington's encampment during the previous winter at Valley Forge may have received more publicity, but the hardships endured by the men of the Redding encampment were equally severe.

Israel Putnam was the senior major general of the Continental Army at the time of the encampment at Redding. Affectionately called "Old Put" by his men, it was he who persuaded army leaders that the base at Redding was a

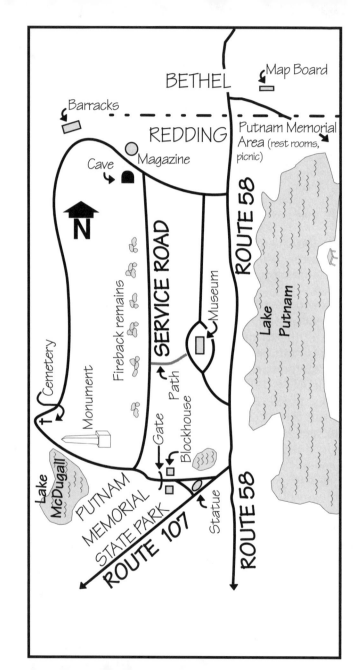

TRAIL TIPS

Picnic areas and out-houses are located in the portion of the park near Lake Putnam (not the historic portion). Bring along refreshments as there are no concessions available. A related site of interest is Walk 53, Putnam Wolf Den. Do note that the memorial park gate (near the statue) is locked at 5:00 P.M. Parking is then limited to spaces near the entrance.

logical and strategic military position. (Meet up with "Old Put" again on Walk 53, Putnam Wolf Den, for another episode in the life of this remarkable man.)

The fight for independence was on. The British were entrenched in New York and continued to harass the colonists in Connecticut. The previous year the soldiers of King George III had attacked and burned Danbury, a major supply depot for the army. From the Redding encampment, Old Put contended, his men could defend the heart of Connecticut and help protect the southeastern coast of the state, the western area, and be prepared to return to the Hudson River in the event of an attack.

To reach Putnam Memorial, follow convenient routes to the junction of Route 107 with Route 58 in Redding. The entrance to the campground is directly west of the junction and is dominated by a dynamic, larger-than-life bronze equestrian statue, created by sculptor Ann Hyatt Huntington when she was 94. The horse and rider depict the general as he made his dramatic mounted escape from pursing British dragoons, down the one hundred steps carved into the precipice at Horse Neck, Greenwich, 1779.

The main gate is flanked by two high blockhouses guarding the gateway. Enter the gate and ascend to the crest of a hill past an obelisk made of native granite, measuring 10 feet square at the base and 40 feet in height, crowned by a huge cannonball. The face of the monument is inscribed ERECTED TO COMMEMORATE THE WINTER QUARTERS OF PUTNAM'S DIVISION OF THE CONTINENTAL ARMY NOVEMBER 7, 1778–MAY 25, 1779.

The memorial shaft is at the beginning of the actual encampment, which is studded with mound after mound of rock piles. These are the fallen chimneys and walls—or firebacks—left where they tumbled from soldier's huts. There is much of historic interest here, including a reconstructed guard house, the 12-by-16-foot log hut that housed twelve men, an officer's hut, Phillip's Cave, a cemetery, and a powder magazine.

A visit to the museum is a must. It is built on the site of the original picket post from which sentries observed the comings and goings of the area. Inside the museum is a display of items uncovered on an archaeological excavation—including a portion of a pipestem, buttons, and a lock. A collection of wooden tools is also of interest.

You may drive the service roads to get a quick overall view; then park your car and wander on foot to the various points of interest. You may observe an ongoing excavation that will continue to add information about the encampment.

Nearby, just a short jog north on Route 58 is a picnic area in the park. Here are views of Lake Putnam, picnic benches, and rest rooms. A map board with details of both park areas is located just inside the entrance.

Sherwood Island

Westport

Explore the Westwood Nature Trail or just wander at a leisurely pace along a 1.25-mile long beach on Long Island Sound through groves and over marshlands. Winter is the ideal time to visit, and this walk is suitable for all abilities.

Connecticut has many firsts to her credit, among them Sherwood Island State Park in Westport. Established in 1914, it was the first state park in Connecticut, one of the first state parks in the nation, and is the only shoreline state park in Fairfield County. Composed of 234 acres of sandy beach, marshes, groves of linden and maple trees, picnic facilities, and a spacious modern pavilion, the park's major feature is the long sweeping beach, bounded by Long Island Sound to the south.

The area was used in season by Native Americans and early settlers arrived in 1648, following the end of the Pequot War. Legend has it that Captain Kidd, the notorious pirate, used the island as a rendezvous point.

The park was named in honor of the Sherwood family, early settlers here who migrated from England's Sherwood Forest, legendary home to Robin Hood and his band of followers.

The entrance to the park may be reached by following routes to exit 18 off the Connecticut Turnpike, Interstate

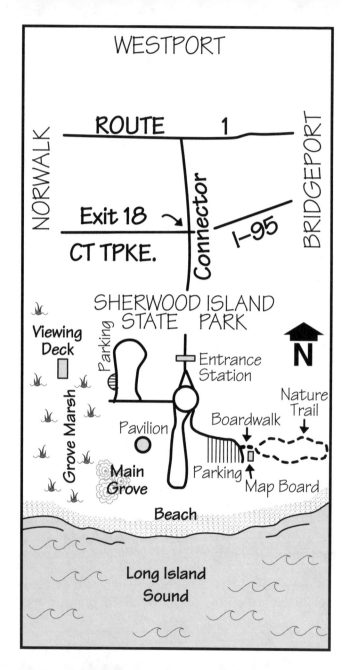

95, in Westport. From exit 18, turn south onto the Sherwood Island Connector and follow it .6 mile to the park gatehouse; then park in a designated area.

Since it is better to walk with a purpose than to meander aimlessly, this walk should start at the far eastern end of the park's beach. Walking close to the edge of the foaming sea as it ebbs and flows can be a fascinating experience.

Explore the shoreline as you go; continue west on the beach to a fence at the western edge of the park. Turn right, leaving the beach, to enter a picnic grove on higher ground. The grove rises a few feet above the surrounding marsh; this higher area provides a vantage point and observation post for bird watchers. When conditions are favorable and with proper footgear, the marsh may be investigated with care.

TRAIL TIPS

Outhouses are available in this popular park, as well as plentiful parking. Admission is charged in season, when the park gets crowded. Food is available in nearby Westport. The nature walk area offers a map board and trail guides. *Note:* Dogs are not allowed April 15 to September 30.

After the walk you may wish to go on the roof deck of the pavilion for a panoramic view of the park grounds, Long Island Sound, and on a clear day, Manhattan skyscrapers. Should the weather be too blustery to picnic comfortably at an outside table, there is a protective glass screen on the pavilion's lower level. This mammoth picture window provides a pleasant outlook to the sound and also affords unexpected warmth when the sun shines through it.

A small boardwalk leads into the nature walk area from the far East Parking Lot. Amtrak trains pass nearby and the roar of Interstate 95 traffic can be heard at the park marshes.

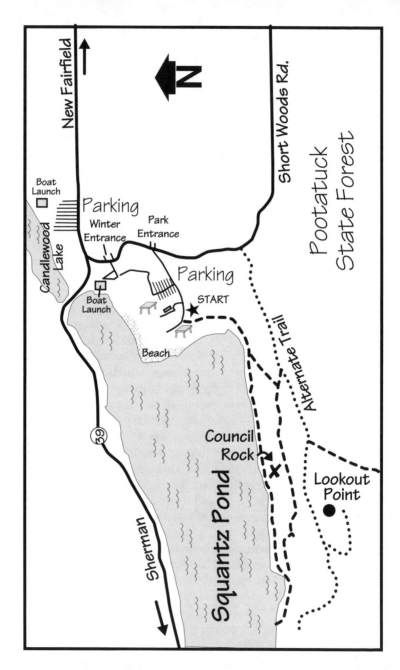

Squantz Pond
New Fairfield

A lakeside walk along wooded paths in the shade of a massive mountain. Off season provides the best opportunity for a quiet walk and observation of water birds, as this park is very popular in summer.

Squantz Pond in the Pootatuck State Forest has setting, beauty, and facilities to suit every taste—the main attraction being the pond itself. There are sandy beaches for children, deeper waters for stronger swimmers, and one may also fish, boat, water ski, picnic, or just relax.

Squantz Pond is an arm of the beautiful Candlewood Lake, the largest body of water within the state. Candlewood Lake is so called because Indians made torches from the resinous pine that grew here. The lake was created in 1928 by the Connecticut Light and Power Company's hydroelectric dam, built on Rocky River in New Milford. The lake covers 10 square miles. Marinas abound in the area.

Bathhouse, beaches, lots of parking, picnic areas, and boat launches make this a popular park. The park is named for Chief Squantz, sachem of the Pootatuck Indians. The tribe frequented this land for hunting, fishing, and held powwows with nearby tribes on a ledge called Council Rock. Many Indian artifacts have reportedly been found amid the rugged hills that surround the park. A walk off-season, when the park is quieter, makes it easier to imagine these pre-colonial times.

The entrance to Squantz Pond State Park is off Route 39 in New Fairfield. Approaching from the south at the intersection of Routes 37 and 39, and in New Fairfield, turn north onto Route 39 and follow it 3.8 miles to the entrance. From the north, at the junction of Routes 37 and 39 in Sherman, take Route 39 south approximately 6 miles to the park entrance west of the highway.

Enter the gate and park in one of the designated areas. The first lot you'll pass is for boaters only. The hiking trails start from the west side of the parking area. The main trail starts at the north end of the picnic area and follows the edge of the pond's western shoreline. Trails and sidepaths are not blazed but are so worn and well defined as to make them easy to follow. Keeping close to the water's edge, go north to the first of four major streams, splashing down several hundred feet from the mountain above to the pond (more of a lake in appearance) below. Crossing the stream, follow the main path along the water's edge, always bearing right.

There are many side trails along the route and you may certainly explore them. Though the trails are not blazed, you needn't worry about getting lost. The pond is always visible and you have only to walk toward the water to pick up the main trail that parallels the shoreline.

TRAIL TIPS

Facilities available include a bathhouse with toilets and off-season outhouses. There are also picnic sites located in the park. Dogs are not allowed May 1 to September 30 in the park area. A small, hiker's parking lot is located near the exit. An entrance fee is charged until the end of September. Trail food or after-trail meals are available in nearby Danbury.

Before investigating any side trails, it would be advisable to stay on the main path past two other streams, the last of which is about 1.5 miles from the picnic area. From the third stream the trail is less trodden but nevertheless visible and easy to follow to a small peninsula with an unobstructed view of the entire waters. This spot is about 2 miles from the start and is an ideal place to rest before returning to your vehicle.

The trail is strewn with huge boulders, tumbled helter-skelter from the high and massive rocky ridge that rises almost directly from the pond's edge to a height of more than 400 feet. A loop trail to Council Rock is worthy of an afternoon expedition, or choose a more strenuous route to Lookout Point. Depending on the amount of time and energy you have to spend, explore the streams and side trails, where numerous caves can be found.

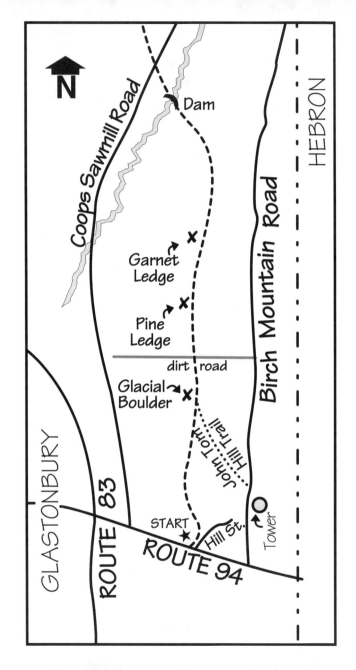

N

Coops Sawmill Road

Dam

HEBRON

Birch Mountain Road

Garnet
Ledge

×

Pine
Ledge

×

dirt road

Glacial
Boulder

×

John Tom Hill Trail

GLASTONBURY

ROUTE 83

START

Hill St.

Tower

ROUTE 94

Glacial Boulders

Glastonbury

A walk through wooded paths, including some uphill scrambles, scenic views, interesting garnet-studded ledges.

All of Connecticut was covered with a vast sheet of ice during the glacial period. Evidence of the great glacier's action is everywhere in the state. An interesting deposit of glacial boulders may be found on the Shenipsit Trail in the town of Glastonbury.

For the starting point of the trail portion that passes through the glacial boulder area, drive to the intersection of Hebron Avenue (Route 94) and Hill Street (a dirt road). This intersection is 2.7 miles east of the intersection of Routes 94 and 83; it is .1 mile west of the intersection of Route 94 and Birch Mountain Road, which is 2.4 miles west of the intersection of Routes 85 and 94. (You can park along Hill Street, but be sure not to block this one-lane road.)

TRAIL TIPS

No rest rooms. Small pull-off for parking near the trail start.

The blue-blazed Shenipsit Trail heads north on Hill Street, then enters the woods on the left at .14 mile. There is a small dirt pull-off located near the entrance to the trail where you can park your car. The trail enters the woods and follows along an old stone wall to the edge of a field and climbs gradually to the top of a ridge at .34 mile. It then continues through the woods, passing under power lines at .53 mile. At .75 mile the path reaches a large glacial boulder and a trail junction. The area is strewn with boulders of every size and variety.

At the junction, the John Tom Hill Trail, marked with blue and white, goes to the right. This side trail will descend steeply, cross a brook, pass under the power lines, and continue through woods to reach Birch Mountain Road, .44 mile from the junction and .1 mile north of a tower.

Many side paths criss-cross the main trail; be sure to periodically check for blue blazes to ensure you are walking on the correct path. Mountain-bike enthusiasts frequent this section of the woods; keep alert for their passage.

Along your journey, note the scab-like lichens that cling to the boulders. Called "time stains," these slow-growing life forms may be hundreds of years old. Recent rain or snow will freshen their appearance. Mountain laurel and wild blueberry shrubs are abundant along the path. The delicate blossom of the mountain laurel is Connecticut's state flower; the shrub blooms in the spring and is a relation of the garden rhododendron. Also note the sometimes thick veins of quartz that are visible in the twisted outcroppings of ancient rock. They resemble toothpaste that has been squeezed into rock crevices.

The Shenipsit Trail descends from the boulder-strewn ridge to a small, swampy area and a road just north of the swamp. From the road, the trail ascends gradually and then steeply for a short distance to Pine Ledge, with a fair view of Hartford, which is visible through the trees to the west. This is a fine area for lunch or a snack; be sure to pack up and take your leftovers with you when you leave. Leaving Pine Ledge, the trail descends through a sag before climbing to the top of Garnet Ledge, almost 2 miles from the start of the walk. The ledge was so named because it and many of the boulders are studded with tiny, pencil-tipped–garnets. Look closely at the rock underfoot and you will see the garnets practically everywhere. Garnets are reddish in color, and minuscule loose stones that have washed out from the rock can be found in the sand.

The round-trip to Garnet Ledge is less than 4 miles. Should you wish to go farther, you may follow the self-guiding trail northwest to an old dam, then to Roaring Brook, before reaching Coops Sawmill Road, less than 3 miles from the start (about 6 miles round-trip). Birdlife is abundant along the trail. Various types of hawks frequent the updrafts east of Pine Ledge and can be seen circling on air currents.

As you walk this trail, you will become aware that, even though you appear to be on high ground, you are actually completely surrounded by much higher hills. Very likely the crags and rugged peaks of the surrounding mountains were bulldozed by the gigantic mass of ice, which then held the rough rocks in its grasp for centuries, grinding and shaping them into the forms in which we now see them. As the ice sheet melted, the captive mellowed stones were released many miles from their origin.

It is estimated that these boulders were dumped in this area approximately 20,000 years ago. All of Connecticut was drastically changed by the work of the great glacier. Geologists guess that the ice at its peak was more than 1,000 feet thick on top of the New Haven area and that it exerted a pressure of 50,000 pounds per square foot on everything it passed over.

Its advance and retreat obliterated old land and rivers, creating new lands and bodies of water. Thanks to the work of the glacier, our state is blessed with a total of 1,026 lakes and 420 swamps.

6

Manituck Lookout
Suffield

This steady uphill walk will lead you to mountain outlooks atop traprock ridges overlooking a valley and far-flung mountains. Children and others might become discouraged by the length as the trail winds steadily upward.

Native Americans who lived in the central Connecticut valley named the northernmost ridge in the state *Amantuck*, meaning "to see in the distance." Today the mountain is called Manituck, and this walk takes you to fine views of that far-flung mountain.

The blue-blazed Metacomet Trail follows a traprock range running from Meriden to the Massachusetts line. The Indian after whom it was named, Metacomet, was also called King Philip. Philip (1639–1676), used the high ridges as strategic outlooks; he oversaw the burning of Simsbury from the heights of Talcott Mountain.

TRAIL TIPS

No facilities are available. Parking is off the side of a sometimes busy road. Suffield has trail supplies and food offerings.

The section of the trail south of Route 168 has fine outlooks over ridges and valleys along a 2-mile stretch that begins at Phelps Street in the town of Suffield.

Phelps Street is on the west side of Route 168 about 3

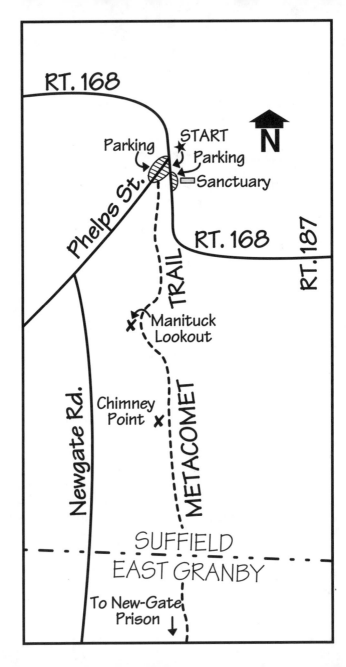

miles east of Congamond Lake. The juncture of Phelps Street with Route 168 is 2.1 miles west of the intersection of Routes 168 and 187 in West Suffield.

Park your car in the vicinity of Phelps Street or off the road near the Howard Wells Alcorn Wildlife Preserve on Route 168. (Use care crossing the road, which can get busy.) Follow the blue-blazed trail west on Phelps Street for .1 mile to where the blazed trail leaves the road to the left (south). Scramble up a steep slope to a woods road, past a sign THE GEORGE A. HARMON WOODLOT, and follow the road till it reaches a traprock ridge affording fine views.

A little more than a mile into the walk, Manituck Lookout offers a view of Manituck Mountain, a forested flat-topped rock mass to the west that is shaped like a pie.

The vantage points along the trail are column-like traprock with rock scree below. The columnar joints appear to have been raked by fingers from cliffs. In late spring wild columbine appears on sunny rock outcrops along the ridge top. Scenery is spectacular with no particular sights other than rolling mountains and valley below.

IN THE AREA

This walk is near Walk 8, Peak Mountain and the historic New-Gate Prison in East Granby.

The trail passes through the Suffield Land Conservancy and a town park, then reaches a traprock crag, Chimney Point, from where the Barndoor Hills and the Western Highlands come into view.

Should you decide to return to your car from here, the round-trip will be approximately 4 miles. Or you may decide to follow the self-guiding trail south a little farther before returning to the starting point.

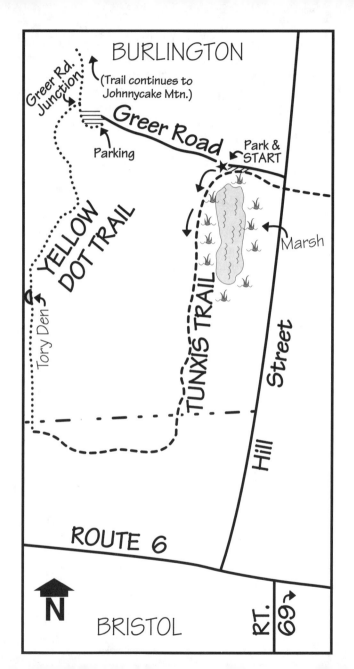

7

Mile of Ledges
Burlington

*A somewhat demanding but rewarding walk past a
swamp and a pond, with interesting rock alleyways, and a
look at the historic Tory Den. Some scrambles and short
climbs are necessary to navigate rock hills. Watch out for
steep drop offs.*

Mile of Ledges is on the Tunxis Trail in the south section
of Burlington, quite near Bristol. The Tunxis offers many
attractions as it meanders over miles of pleasing woodland terrain—among them is one of the steepest miles to
be found on the Connecticut Blue Trail System, historic
Tory Den, as well as Devil's Kitchen Ravine. Mile of
Ledges is said to be the roughest part of the southern
Tunxis Trail.

This area is rich in wildlife, rock ridges, second-growth
forest, and almost meadow-like stretches. Although the
roundtrip is about 3 miles, plan to spend the day here, as
climbing and navigating the rocky crags and exploring
odd alleyways of stone will soak up hours. Along your
journey, enjoy the chipmunks scurrying across fallen
logs, pick out a boulder for a lunch spot, and savor the
silence. Two snakes (both harmless) were spied on a recent walk along with three salamanders, a brightly mot-
tled frog, and a tiny tree frog.

To reach the starting point of this walk, follow the most convenient route to Bristol's combined Route U.S. 6 and Route 69. From Route 69 at the western end of the combined routes, follow Route U.S. 6 west 1.1 miles to Hill Street. Turn north, right, onto Hill Street and follow it 3 miles to Greer Road. Turn northwest, left, onto Greer Road and follow it .2 mile to the western edge of a large swamp/pond, where the trail leaves the road to enter woodland. Park your car off the shoulder of the road, and follow a blazed trail south over undulating terrain, ascending gradually to the Mile of Ledges.

TRAIL TIPS

No facilities are available near the trail. Parking is limited at the trail's start; there are areas to park located farther up Greer Road near the end of the trail loop. Nearby Bristol has food places aplenty.

At about .5 mile from Greer Road, you will encounter one towering ledge after another. At about 1.10 miles you'll encounter a stone dam wall foundation with the center now torn down that once crossed the U-shaped valley. Once crossed over there are blocks and blocks of rock to clamber over and up.

The Yellow Dot Trail, which is marked by a blue blaze with a yellow dot in its center, is about 1.35 miles from the start. At the junction of the main blue-blazed Tunxis Trail with the Yellow Dot Trail, turn north, right, and follow the Yellow Dot Trail to historic Tory Den, about .2 mile. The den is located right off the side of the trail.

The Tory Den is an historic landmark; it was used as a hideout during the Revolutionary War by the Tories of the area when they were too hotly pressed by overzealous Patriots. Today the den, actually a tunnel beneath rock, continues to offer sanctuary, peace, and solitude to those who would flee momentarily the press of civilization. A nearby rock shelter (left of trail) with blackened-by-soot walls shows evidence of past campfires. The den was one of the stopovers reportedly used by the Old Leatherman (see Leatherman Cave, Walk 18).

From Tory Den the Yellow Dot Trail continues north just over a mile to Greer Road Junction. Turn right, descend to Greer Road, and follow the road approximately .5 mile to your parked car.

Note: At the end of the Yellow Dot Trail, dogs should be leashed and under control to ensure the continued use of the trail over private land. The suburban neighborhood along the road makes for a pleasant stroll to return to your vehicle.

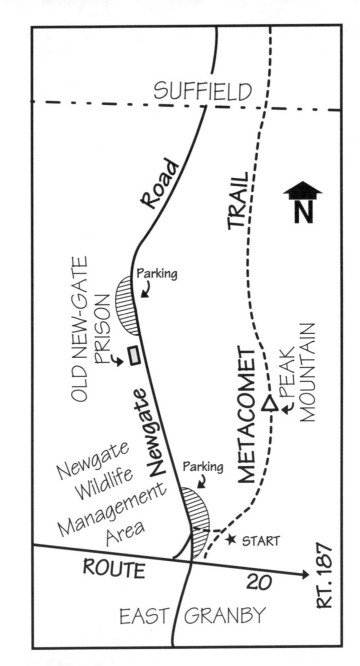

8

Peak Mountain

East Granby

Hike up the side of Peak Mountain to the highest point on the Metacomet Trail between Tariffville and the Massachusetts state line. The trail is rocky in spots, but it's not too tiring if you pace it. There are good views and it is a popular spot on autumn foliage weekends.

Peak Mountain is 672 feet above sea level and offers exceptional views; a bonus is that it is quite near a historic site, Old New-Gate Prison.

Access to the trail that leads up Peak Mountain may be easily reached from either Route 190 in Suffield or Route 20 in East Granby. The shortest approach is from Route 20 on the south. To reach this point, follow the most convenient route to the intersection of Routes 20 and 187 at East Granby. Follow Route 20 west .6 mile to Newgate Road, on the right. On Route 20 near the corner is a standard blue-and-white oval sign indicating the Metacomet Trail. The walk starts nearby.

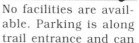
TRAIL TIPS

No facilities are available. Parking is along trail entrance and can get crowded. Bring along trail food; there's not much available in the area for supplies.

Park your car alongside Newgate Road (a popular spot, especially in autumn) and follow the trail north up a very steep wooded slope. Numerous unmarked trails join up with the blue-blazed trail from the parking area. Stone outcrops poke through the leaf litter and underbrush. The trail continues north on the crest of the ridge, with fine views to the east and west. Peak Mountain is reached 1 mile from Route 20; the trail leads north along the crest of Peak Mountain through hardwood forest to Turkey Hills Lookout, at approximately 1.3 miles from the starting point. You may wish to rest and picnic here while enjoying the distant views. Should you desire to go farther, continue on the blazed trail north, returning from any point you decide upon.

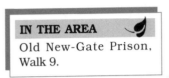

IN THE AREA

Old New-Gate Prison, Walk 9.

There is an extra bonus that may be enjoyed together with this walk to Peak Mountain. This section of the Metacomet Trail parallels Newgate Road, on which Old New-Gate Prison is located. It is only 1.2 miles north from Route 20 to the crumbling remains of what was once a busy copper mine and later a state prison and a federal jail.

9

Old New-Gate Wildlife Trail

East Granby

This is a wonderful walk that can be combined with a visit to the historic Old New-Gate Prison for a memorable day trip.

Old New-Gate Prison, with crumbling ruins above ground and the tunnels of the mine below, is quite fascinating. The prison is state property and is open to the public. Its history began in 1705, when it was known as Copper Hill and the first mining probe for copper was started. In 1707 a group of land proprietors of Simsbury formed the first company to work the mines.

In 1773 the Colony of Connecticut first used the tunnels and caverns 30 feet below the surface as a permanent prison. It was during the American Revolution that the title of the prison was changed to New-Gate after Newgate Prison of London, England. In

TRAIL TIPS

There are rest rooms inside the visitor center as well as vending machines. Admission is charged, but the ground and nature walk are free. An interpretive nature trail is open May 15 through October 14. The parking lot closes at 4:30 P.M. A three-dimensional relief map tablet is located on the park grounds and depicts the major mountains and peaks of the Farmington Valley.

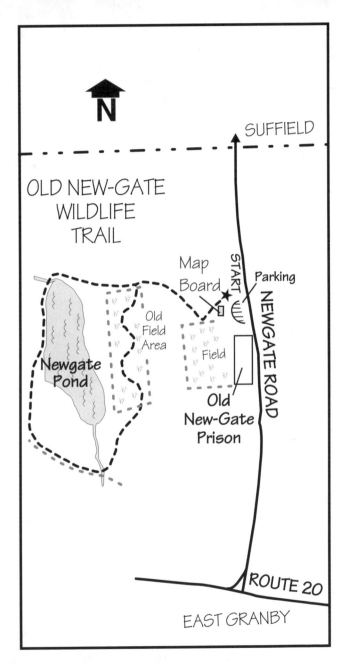

1781 Congress made New-Gate of Connecticut a government jail for prisoners of war. During its fifty-four years as a prison, many British, Tory, and state prisoners were kept in the dank, dark dungeons. As many as forty prisoners at one time were confined in the rock-hewn holes, and they were compelled to work in the mine and workshops. In the 1820s female prisoners were sent to Newgate, but they were kept in cells above ground.

After 1827, when Wethersfield was made a state prison site, Old New-Gate Prison was abandoned.

Reach the historic site from either Route 190 in Suffield or Route 20 in East Granby. The shortest approach is from Route 20 on the south. To reach this point follow the most convenient route to the intersection of Routes 20 and 187 at East Granby. Follow Route 20 west .6 mile to Newgate Road, on the right. Travel north on Newgate Road until you reach the site; parking is on the left, just past the signs. The walk starts from the parking lot, near a map board that gives details about the walk.

IN THE AREA

This walk is near Manituck Outlook, Walk 6, and Walk 8, Peak Mountain.

The trail is a .8-mile walk that begins near the prison and illustrates wildlife habitat management practices, old field growth, and ways in which plantings can attract birds. The views of the Farmington Valley are breathtaking.

The gentle walk is maintained by the state DEP Wildlife Division and is operated in conjunction with the Connecticut Historical Commission, which oversees the New-Gate Prison. The path leads through woods to the edge of a field, bends along the old field area, and past Newgate Pond. A detailed brochure about the vegetation and wildlife is available from a map board at the start of the walk or from the visitor's center, when it is open.

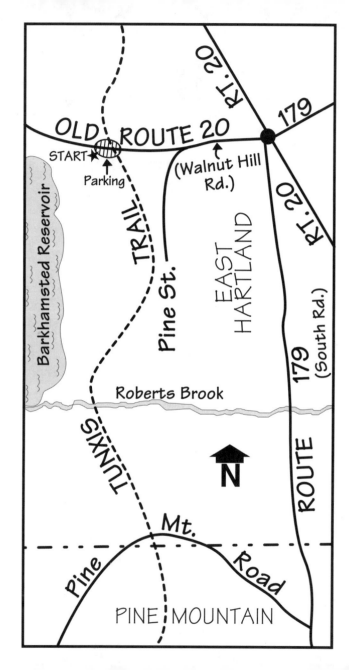

10

Roberts Brook
Hartland

Hike through peaceful woods along a winding trail past water and fields. Suitable for most abilities and ages, with some inclines.

Quiet woods are a sanity saver and restorative after the hum and frenzy of modern life.

The Tunxis Trail passes through Hartland between and paralleling the Barkhamsted Reservoir and the Hartland–Granby boundary line. Roberts Brook is crossed by the trail approximately 1.75 miles south of old Route 20 and about .75 mile north of Pine Mountain in Barkhamsted.

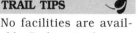

TRAIL TIPS

No facilities are available. Parking is along an unused road. Use caution while driving on the road as it is rutted and has many potholes. Bring refreshments as there are no food stops in the immediate area. This walk starts right across from the Walk 11, Tunxis State Forest.

To reach the start of the walk, drive to the intersection of Route 20, Route 179, and Old Route 20 (Walnut Hill Road) in East Hartland. Follow Old Route 20. About a mile from this intersection, Pine Street goes left. Keep following Walnut Hill Road straight into the forest. About .25 mile into the forest, the blue-blazed

Tunxis Trail crosses the old road; this walk starts on the left side of the road. (For a walk heading in the opposite direction, see Walk 11, Tunxis State Forest.) Use care on the road as it is pocked with holes.

Park your car and follow the self-guiding trail south, ascending immediately to a crest. The trail dips and rises over several hills and shortly reaches a barbed wire fence on the west, which it clings to for some of the way. Use care when following this trail; there are deceptive paths and woods roads that tend to lead one astray. Be sure to have a blue blaze in view before advancing too far.

Roberts Brook is reached at just under 2 miles. The trail continues south for about .75 mile to Pine Mountain Road and the north base of Pine Mountain. You may return to your car after reaching Roberts Brook or extend your walk by going on to Pine Mountain for a fine view of Springfield before returning.

Tunxis State Forest
Hartland

A blissful walk through quiet woods over a cobbled stream with small waterfalls. An afternoon can easily be passed enjoying the beauty of these woods. Suitable for most ages and abilities as the trail winds over varied rolling terrain including meadows edged by stone walls.

At the northern end of the Tunxis Trail, near its terminus at the Massachusetts state line, are some exceptional walks.

One of the most rewarding segments of the trail is between Old Route 20 and Route 20 in Hartland. The walk, within the boundaries of Tunxis State Forest, is less than 5 miles round trip.

TRAIL TIPS

No facilities are available here. Parking is in a pull-off on an unused road. Bring along trail treats as there aren't any stores nearby.

To reach the start drive to the intersection of Route 20, Route 179, and Old Route 20 (Walnut Hill Road) in East Hartland. Follow Old Route 20 straight into the forest (about 1 mile beyond the intersection with Pine Street on the left). Use care as the old paved road is now pocked with holes. At about .25 mile into the forest, the blue-blazed Tunxis Trail crosses the old road.

This walk starts on the right side; for a walk heading the other direction, see Walk 10, Roberts Brook.

The trail soon crosses a delightful brook, then continues a short distance before descending into a glade and another, livelier brook that flows into the Barkhamsted Reservoir. After crossing the brook and exploring the small waterfalls and dark pools, continue on the trail as it winds past a logged area and ascends gradually to a dirt road. Follow the road briefly, then walk the easy path through a meadow area to reach Route 20 at about 2 miles from the start.

Return from here and retrace your steps to the dirt road where the trail reenters woods to the left, south. The dirt road was at one time the approach to a ski slope, once popular but now abandoned. The road is now used only as a part of an occasional cross-country ski run and as an approach to a cabin at the western end.

The state-owned log cabin (reserved exclusively for use by Boy Scout troops) is at the dead end of the dirt road about .25 mile west of the blue-blazed crossing. Although off the main part of the trail, a side trip will prove to be an extra bonus and leads through an area fringed with ferns, accented with lichen-encrusted stone walls. (Lichen only grows where the air and water is clean; pollution kills it.)

This is an ideal spot to picnic and rest, enjoying the silence. Chipmunks abound in the area and love to perch on the stone walls, often scampering across the trail with their tails held straight up like rudders.

Returning from the site, follow the road east to the blazed trail, then back to your car.

The land now known as the Tunxis State Forest was probably never occupied or controlled by the Tunxis Indians, who were a subtribe of the Sicaogs. Grand Sachem Sequassen ruled both tribes. The Sicaogs claimed the area that is now Hartford and West Hartford, while the Tunxis tribe settled in the Farmington area, including much of the surrounding land.

The Indian name for the Farmington River was Tunxis, which is an abbreviation for *Tunxisepo*, also *Tunch-seasapose*. Both of these forms are short for Watunk-shausepo, which means "fast-flowing and winding river."

IN THE AREA

For a walk in the oppo-site direction, see Walk 10, Roberts Brook.

It is supposed to have de-scribed the sharp bend in the Farmington River where its flow changes abruptly from a southeasterly to a northerly course. It was quite natural that a tribe living in the Farm-ington River Valley became known as the Tunxis Indians.

What is now state forest was in all probability a part of the land in the northwest corner of Connecticut never per-manently settled by any Indians. This was a sort of no-man's land, constantly fought over by the Mohawks of New York and the Tunxis of Connecticut, both claiming the rich hunting ground as their own.

12

Dinosaur State Park

Rocky Hill

A walk that can be made any time during the year and that all ages can enjoy. Choose a circuitous loop or walk across a boardwalk, especially wonderful in the spring when frogs and new flowers may be seen. In summer, explore the theme gardens.

Connecticut has its own Jurassic Park. Well, sort of. Located near the center of the state is Rocky Hill and Dinosaur State Park, the largest enclosed and interpreted dinosaur trackway in North America.

The fossil imprints were discovered in 1966 during excavation for a building. The remarkable site then became a 10-acre state park. More than 200 species of plant families and trees grow on the grounds. An added bonus is the developed gardens of native wildflowers, grasses, and 2.5 miles of nature trails.

To reach the park, follow routes to Rocky Hill. The park is located 1 mile east of Exit 23 off I–91. Park in the designated area and walk to the beginning of trails, where information may be obtained.

In this beautiful setting, it's possible to roam through woods across a swamp boardwalk and imagine the days when the trackmaker called Eubrontes, named the official state fossil, roamed the earth millions of years ago.

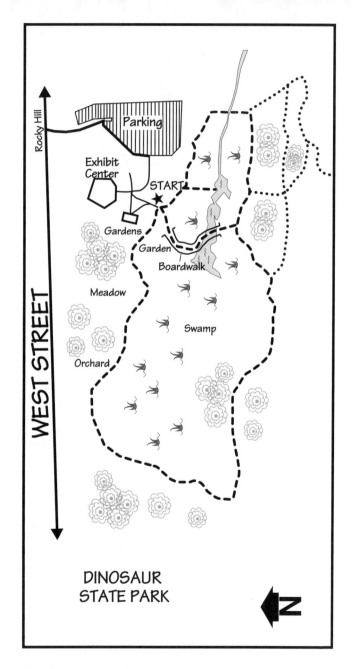

Parking

Rocky Hill

Exhibit
Center

START

Gardens

Garden
Boardwalk

Meadow

Swamp

Orchard

WEST STREET

DINOSAUR
STATE PARK

N

No skeletal remains of the animal that created the bird-like imprints have yet been discovered. Scientists believe Eubrontes was similar to the Dilphosaurus, a large carnivorous dinosaur in the Jurassic period.

At the time of the dinosaurs, the area was part of a lake-plain with muddy conditions that were ideal for making the tracks. A traprock ridge and broken chunks of basaltic rock located in the park speak of the hot lava that eventually covered the watery habitat of the dinosaurs.

Only a small portion of the trackway is on display under the geodesic dome exhibit center; much of the fossilized imprints remain buried for protection.

This is a perfect family walk that all ages can enjoy year-round. Varied natural history (birds, star-gazing, wildlife) walks are offered as well; check for schedules. You may choose to hike a circuitous loop or the 300-foot-long boardwalk area, especially of interest in the spring when frogs and spring flowers may be seen with ease. In summer explore the butterfly garden—a special treat, especially with very young children.

TRAIL TIPS

Parking is available on a hard-surface lot. Admission to the park is free, but a fee is charged to tour the indoor center exhibits. Rest rooms are located inside. The center is closed Monday, but the trails remain open. Plaster casts of tracks may be made at the park, May 1 to October 31; call for hours and details about the supplies you'll need to bring. Rocky Hill and nearby Cromwell have eateries and places to buy food for a trailside picnic.

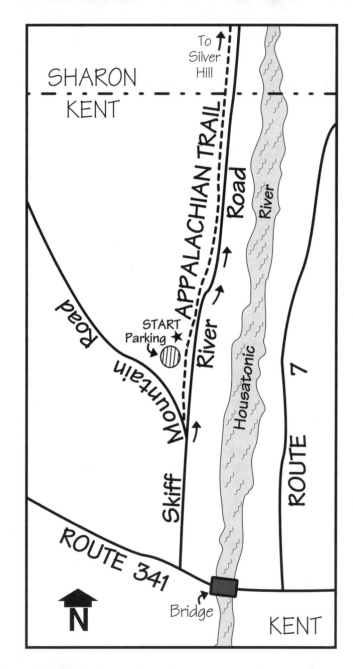

13

River Road

Kent

A level, pleasant riverside walk on a section of the Appalachian Trail offers quiet water to explore in summer. Varied environments provide homes to all sorts of wildflowers, birds, insects, and small mammals. In fall the foliage is spectacular. Suitable for all abilities.

The 53-mile stretch of Appalachian Trail in Connecticut is mostly steep and rugged terrain. In contrast there are a few sections of this trail that are more or less level and relatively easy to walk. One such section is the 5-mile stretch along the west bank of the Housatonic River between St. John's Ledges in Kent and Silver Hill in Sharon.

Drive to the intersection of Routes 7 and 341 in the center of Kent. From the intersection follow Route 341 west across the Housatonic River Bridge to Skiff Mountain Road. It is the first road to the right, west of the river. Turn north onto Skiff Mountain Road and follow it 1.1 miles to the junction with River Road. Skiff Mountain Road bears left here. Follow River Road to its end, where the foot trail that is a section of the Appalachian Trail begins.

Park your car in the small grassy lot and follow the white-blazed Appalachian Trail north as it parallels the wide, easy-flowing Housatonic River. Trail and road cling close to the river on the east. (The parking area is at the end of River Road, about a mile past St. John's Ledge, where River Road ends.

Numerous streams tumble down the face of the mountain range and flow into the Housatonic in this area. The river and the mountain streams along this portion of the Appalachian Trail have an eye-appeal unmatched by sights from higher elevations. Wet, icy, or snowy conditions, however, can make it very difficult to follow this trail.

TRAIL TIPS

An outhouse is located near the start of the trail. The river is popular for fishing and summer outings. The village of Kent has several family-style restaurants and an ice cream/sandwich shop. Sections of this trail are on or close to state forest land and private land open to hunting. Hikers should wear blaze orange and be aware of deer season (check dates in autumn). This walk is near Walk 14, Macedonia Brook State Park.

At the end of River Road, where the foot traffic only is allowed (no bikes, horses, or vehicles are permitted), trail maps are available from a small wooden box attached to a towering sycamore tree. Walks may be tailored to ability and desire. A very pleasant day may be passed exploring along the wide and shallow river. (Be aware that heavy rains or spring snow melts can turn the river into fast-moving waters.)

The trail is shaded and wide with oceans of ferns, bee balm, and wildflowers. Massive trees line the banks. During the summer crayfish scuttle among the river-smoothed rocks. Tracks of deer and the tiny imprints of their accompanying fawns, alongside blue heron tracks (they resemble dinosaur prints), and the hand-like prints of raccoons dot the many sandbars. A cloud of butterflies can be glimpsed as it takes to the air from a resting spot along a quiet river cove. Be sure to tuck in a pair of shoes (thick-soled sandals) for wading into the river.

Birdlife is abundant; Canada geese and mallards share the river with hikers and sunbathers. The distinctive clattering call of the belted kingfisher can be heard. This area has been named one of the ten best birding spots in Connecticut. In autumn the sky and blazing foliage on the mountains reflected in the river water are stunning.

The river walk continues for about 5 miles to Silver Hill. (There the trail goes on up the hill, then descends sharply.) You may walk the entire distance or shorten your walk to whatever length you wish.

The Connecticut section of the Appalachian Trail is maintained by volunteers from the Connecticut chapter of the Appalachian Mountain Club. While out on the trail consider that it is possible (should you wish) to keep walking this path north to Maine, or turn around and tramp southward all the way to Georgia. The trails committee that helps maintain this section of the AT asks that hikers observe a few simple rules: Carry out what you carry in; fires are allowed in the designated areas only; use the facilities/bathrooms available on the trail. This section of the AT sees heavy use as a recreational area; help the volunteers keep it in good shape.

The AT is 2,150 miles long and passes through fourteen states. Work on the national scenic trail started in

IN THE AREA

Of interest is the Sloane-Stanley Museum and Kent Iron Works, located just north of Kent. This is a great spot for a picnic with interesting facets of the area's history explained at the site.

1921 and was completed in 1937.

While out walking look for hikers with an AMC patch; it identifies guides who can provide information about the trail. You may even see a through-hiker—a person who is walking the complete trail from Georgia to Maine in one fell swoop.

14

Cobble Mountain

Kent

This challenging walk leads up a steep trail. It has numerous switchbacks, boulders, and a sometimes tough climb uphill. Once on top, there are breathtaking views of seemingly endless mountain ranges. Cobble Mountain is the highest viewpoint in this area.

Macedonia Brook State Park is in the town of Kent. Cobble Mountain, on the Macedonia Ridge Trail, is the highest point (1,380 feet) in the area.

The park has a variety of trails, from easy strolls suitable for families with young children to quite strenuous and rugged hikes. There are several loop trails of varying lengths that bring you back to the starting point without retracing your steps. One of these is the white-blazed trail leading to Cobble Mountain.

Macedonia Brook State Park's south entrance may be reached from the intersection of Routes 7 and 341 at the center of Kent. From this intersection drive northwest on Route 341 approximately 1.7 miles to Macedonia Brook Road, which is the main road through the park. Turn north onto this road and follow it to the park entrance, indicated by the sign. About 1 mile from the entrance, the log cabin ranger headquarters is located between Macedonia Brook Road and the old Civilian Conserva-

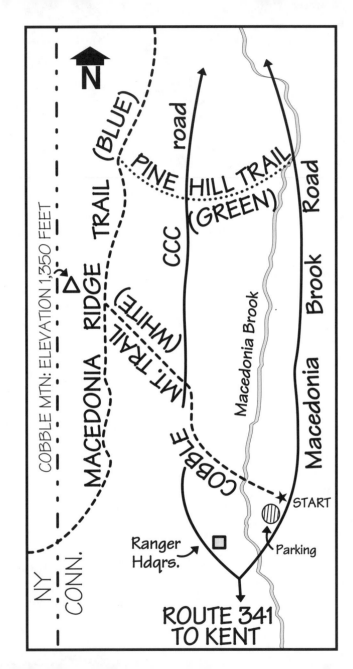

N

COBBLE MTN: ELEVATION 1,350 FEET

MACEDONIA RIDGE TRAIL (BLUE)

PINE HILL TRAIL (GREEN)

road

CCC

Mt. TRAIL (WHITE)

COBBLE

Macedonia Brook

Macedonia Brook Road

NY
CONN.

Ranger Hdqrs.

START

Parking

ROUTE 341
TO KENT

tion Corps (CCC) road, once called Sharon Road, on the left (west).

The white-blazed trail begins on Macedonia Brook Road. It is marked by a sign saying COBBLE MOUNTAIN where it crosses a footbridge, near the pavilion just north of the ranger headquarters. After parking your car, follow the white-blazed trail northwest. The small stream under the bridge is fun to play in, or just sit by it and listen to the waters flow. The trail soon joins the CCC road (dirt and grass) for .2 mile and then turns off, ascending steeply for .4 mile to the juncture with the blue-blazed Macedonia Ridge Trail.

Be forewarned that the Cobble Mountain trail in-

INDIAN PIPES

Along the Cobble Mountain Trail look for the ghostly white Indian pipes, a plant that resembles ceremonial peace pipes used by Native Americans. Indian pipes are approximately 3 inches tall and usually grow in a cluster. They are fragile, but after maturing they turn black, tough and dry; the dried form can be seen year-round. The plant, also called ice plant or corpse plant, grows in rich, shaded woods, never in open sunlight.

—C.B.

---

volves scrambling over rocks and around boulders and tramping uphill using switchbacks. This is a tough trail not suitable for very young children or the faint hearted. Once near the top, follow the blue-blazed trail west (right) to the crest of Cobble Mountain. The view from here is extensive and magnificent. It is one of the finest outlooks in the state with views of multiple ridges and mountain ranges. New York State is visible to the west. For an unforgettable experience, watch the sun dip behind the mountain crests with the clouds aglow. Spend as much time as you wish on the mountaintop, and

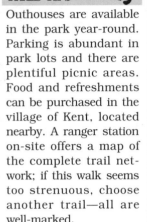

TRAIL TIPS

Outhouses are available in the park year-round. Parking is abundant in park lots and there are plentiful picnic areas. Food and refreshments can be purchased in the village of Kent, located nearby. A ranger station on-site offers a map of the complete trail network; if this walk seems too strenuous, choose another trail—all are well-marked.

when satiated follow the blue-blazed trail .3 mile to the juncture with the green-blazed Pine Hill Trail, which descends south another .3 mile to CCC road, thence south on the CCC road .4 mile to the starting point. Pack a flashlight for the trip down, should you need it, and watch your step. The blue-blazed trail comes down from the mountain over rough and rugged terrain. Although the hazardous portion of this trail is short, it should be negotiated with care. It is advisable not to try this section when it is wet or covered with snow. Under these conditions *do not* try the green-blazed trail. It would be better to retrace the white-blazed trail back to your car, and even this route is best avoided under adverse weather conditions.

Macedonia Brook State Park, composed of 2,294 acres, has an abundance of all those things that appeal to naturalists. Whether your interest is geology, botany, wildlife, hiking, or just a desire for quiet and solitude, you may satisfy it here.

Macedonia Brook flows through 4 miles of picturesque gorge in the heart of the park in Nodine Hollow. The main road passes through the park from Route 341 on the south to the Sharon-Kent boundary line on the north. All but one of the trails start from the main park road. Those to the east are generally less steep than those to the west.

Each trail is blazed with its own color: white, red, yellow, blue, green, or orange. A map showing the various trails and other features may be obtained from the ranger on duty. In season the picnic and campsite areas in the park are very popular. For those who wish to get away from the crowds, winter is the ideal season to visit.

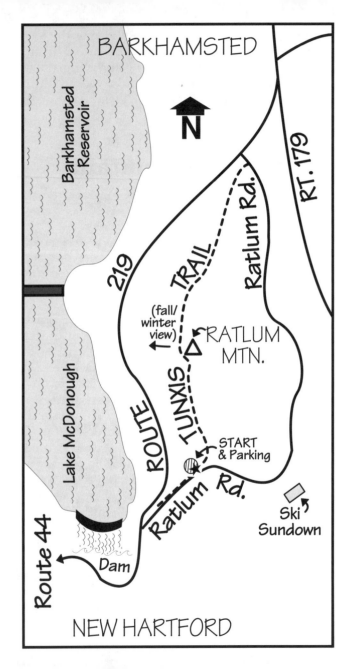

Ratlum Mountain
New Hartford

Climb a mountain on this walk and sign the trail register at the top. The views are the best when the trees are leafless. Most everyone can enjoy this walk; it is not too difficult going uphill if you take your time.

Ratlum Mountain is on the Tunxis Trail of the Connecticut Blue Trail System near the midpoint of Ratlum Road, which begins in New Hartford and ends in Barkhamsted.

Approaching from the south and west, follow the most convenient route to the intersection of Routes 44 and 219 in New Hartford. From the intersection follow Route 219 east 1.5 miles to Ratlum Road in the township of New Hartford.

TRAIL TIPS

No facilities are available. Parking is off the side of the road.

Approaching from the east, drive south to the junction of Route 179 with Route 219 in Barkhamsted. From the junction follow Route 219 southwest 1.5 miles to the north end of Ratlum Road, in the township of Barkhamsted; continue on Route 219 for 3.75 miles to the south end of Ratlum Road, in New Hartford.

Turn northeast onto Ratlum Road, passing Ski Sundown and following blue blazes on trees along the road until the blazed trail enters the woods. Park your car and follow the blazed trail north, passing a barbed wire fence pasture on your right, ascending gradually uphill easily to Ratlum Mountain, less than 1 mile from the starting point. Be sure to sign in at the trail register, placed in a wooden box mounted on a tree at the top.

Silence—what the modern world is lacking—can be found here in abundance, especially on weekdays. When trees are bare there are outstanding views of the valley to the north, Lake McDonough, the Compensating and Barkhamsted reservoirs, and the East Branch of the Farmington River. The rest of the year the leaves obscure the views. In the winter you can see skiers riding up the lifts and zooming down the slopes of Ski Sundown.

The trail continues north from Mount Ratlum 2.5

miles to the Barkhamsted terminus of Ratlum Road. Wild turkeys are frequently spotted along Ratlum Road. The round-trip from one Ratlum terminus to the other is approximately 7 miles. You may do all of it or return from Mount Ratlum or any other point along the trail.

When walking the woodland trails during any season except winter, it is probable that you will see one or more bumblebees. You can call them either "bumble" or "humble" bees, but "bumble" is more common. Both names suggest the humming, buzzing, droning sound made by these insects when in flight. The scientific name of the genus is *Bombus*, Latin for "buzzing" or "humming."

The bumblebee has a large black body covered with a thick fuzzy coat of white or yellow hair. Its flight is not so graceful as that of the honeybee, yet it maneuvers expertly in flight. After examining a bumblebee a scientist once declared that aerodynamically, due to its large body, clumsy design, and small wing surface, it should never be able to fly. Fortunately for us, the bumblebee does not know the rules and miraculously she does fly.

We owe much to the bumblebee for her services as a pollinator of plants. Those flowers with deep corollas, which cannot be reached by the short-tongued honeybee, must be served by the longer-tongued bumblebee.

IN THE AREA

Nearby Collinsville is a worthy day trip with a coffee shop-bookstore, a kayak and canoe center, and quiet streets for strolling. This is a good place to go after the walk.

The bumblebee is a social insect, but, unlike honeybees, the bumblebee colony does not live over winter; only the young pregnant queens survive, coming out of hibernation in the spring to start a new colony.

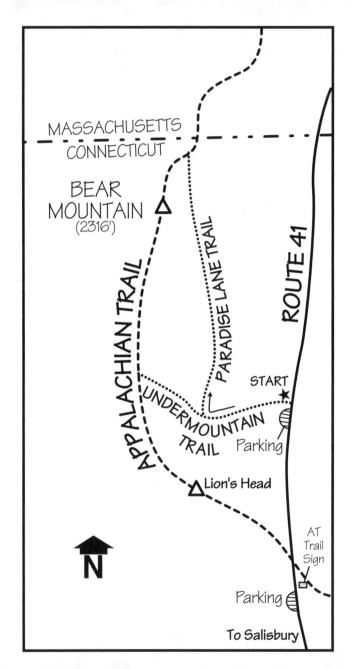

MASSACHUSETTS
CONNECTICUT

BEAR
MOUNTAIN
(2316')

PARADISE LANE TRAIL

APPALACHIAN TRAIL

ROUTE 41

START

UNDERMOUNTAIN
TRAIL

Parking

Lion's Head

N

AT
Trail
Sign

Parking

To Salisbury

16

Bear Mountain
Salisbury

One of the most challenging and rewarding walks in this book—it follows the Appalachian Trail to the peak of Bear Mountain. The day-long, more than 12-mile walk offers the highest scenic outlook in the state and views include a sea of mountain tops.

There is a universal allure about things that have the reputation of being the longest, widest, highest, or any other superlative quality. The highest point in any area seems to have special appeal for the hiker. The highest mountain peak in the world, Mount Everest, has little to offer its conquerors after they suffer the extreme hardships to reach its top, other than the satisfaction of having reached the heights. A simple explanation of this compulsive urge to climb even the smallest hill was given by George Leigh Mallory, who,

TRAIL TIPS

AT trail maps are available at the beginning of the trail, as is an outhouse. For a truly unforgettable walk, try this on a weekday when it is less populated. You should be prepared for this walk: Wear boots, carry adequate water, and allow enough time to reach the summit and return—this is an all-day walk and well worth it.

when asked why he wanted to climb Mount Everest, said, "Because it is there."

Bear Mountain attracts hundreds of hikers to its crest, which is 2,316 feet above sea level. It is the highest mountain peak entirely within the bounds of the state, but, oddly enough, it is not the highest point in the state. Connecticut's highest elevation of 2,380 feet is on the Connecticut–Massachusetts boundary line as it passes over the south shoulder of Mount Frissel, the peak of which is in Massachusetts. Bear Mountain is the highest scenic outlook, however, where you may see a virtual ocean of mountain peaks rippling off to the horizon.

IN THE AREA

The Drugstore Cafe on Main Street in Salisbury has great treats for the trail or afterward. (Try the huge trail cookie!) The Village Store on Main Street has detailed topographical maps, as well as outdoor equipment supplies.

Bear Mountain is in the township of Salisbury and may be reached by numerous trails, the most important of which is the Appalachian Trail (AT).

From the junction of Routes 44 and 41 in the center of Salisbury, follow Route 41 north 3.2 miles to a hiker parking lot on the left. *Note:* You will first pass a parking lot on the left at .8 mile. This lot offers AT access to Lion's Head and is detailed in Walk 17. Drive on to the second parking area at 3.2 miles.

The blue-blazed Undermountain Trail, a popular access trail to the AT, starts here. Follow the Undermountain Trail—which begins to ascend steadily—for a little more than a mile to the Paradise Lane Trail, also blue-blazed, on the right. Take Paradise to go up a plateau, past a swampy area with ferns and a pond, and cross an open ledge to reach the white-blazed AT. Turn left on the AT and soon travel very steep slopes of a ledge.

At the crest of Bear Mountain you'll find a stone monument, blueberry bushes, and misshapen, wind-beaten trees. Along the entire pathway you'll also find great views from outlooks in all directions—the Catskills to the west, Twin Lakes to the east, towering Mount Everett to the north, and Mohawk Mountain to the southeast.

After admiring the views, continue on the white-blazed Appalachian Trail; the rocky path will give way to an old woods road. When you come to the blue-blazed Undermountain Trail on the left, take that to return to the parking lot.

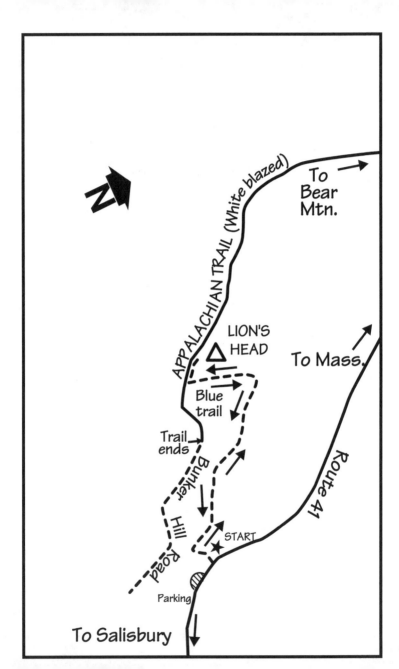

Lion's Head

Salisbury

Leave the crowds behind on this walk across the spine of a mountain. You'll get incredible views of the Berkshires. Quiet woods, massive trees, and outcrops of garnet-studded rock will be found along the trail. An all-day excursion, this is a challenging walk.

Should you choose an all-day expedition with rewarding views of both Lion's Head and Bear Mountain, leave your vehicle at the hikers parking lot at .8 mile out from Salisbury. The lot is just after two signs that depict hikers, where the AT crosses the road (the lot for Bear Mountain is farther north on the same road).

To access the white-blazed AT trail, follow the trail—which ascends gradually, passing through forest with some stupendously large trees. Natural steps of tree roots and stones are underfoot and white birch, many with multiple trunks, are abundant. Glades of hemlock

TRAIL TIPS

This is rugged country; wear sturdy boots and carry adequate water. An outhouse is located near the AT parking lot, .8 mile from the junction of Routes 44 and 41. AT trail maps are available at the start of the walk from the map board.

and maple accent the quiet woods.

Near the top is a rock staircase and junction of trails; continue right on the white-blazed AT to the top of Lion's Head, involving a steep climb up a rock knob. Trails marked blue and white run together now, divide, and then combine again atop the mountain. From the summit is a view of endless mountains, the Berkshire Hills and a view of three states—Connecticut, Massachusetts, and New York.

To the right and left of the trail are outlooks; be sure to investigate both views. Twin Lakes can be seen to the east and Bear Mountain looms ahead to the north.

Choose to continue the walk to Bear Mountain north or return to your vehicle via the same white-blazed route.

Note: Be sure, when retracing your steps down the mountain, to stay on the white-blazed trail—the same one used in ascending. A short section of a blue-blazed

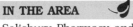

IN THE AREA

Salisbury Pharmacy and the Drugstore Cafe is a great stop for trail cookies or a smoothie. Nearby is Walk 16, Bear Mountain.

trail continues straight ahead as you descend Lion's Head, but does not intersect with the AT and ends at a small road, far from your parked vehicle. A more direct route to Walk 16 Bear Mountain (less than 7 miles one way) is found at 3.2 miles north of the junction of Routes 41 and 44, where the blue-blazed Undermountain Trail leads to the Paradise Lane Trail, then up to the AT and along to the plateau of Bear Mountain.

INSECTS

The universally famous "Homer of Insects," Jean-Henri Fabre, spent a lifetime studying, discovering, and recording the activities of the myriad insect worlds within the confines of his small garden. Extreme poverty prevented Fabre from going places he dreamed about as a boy. Yet his own backyard gave him as much excitement, adventure, pleasure, and perhaps greater fame than he would have gained had his boyhood dreams of travel been realized.

Just one step from our own doorstep, or a few steps farther to the blue-blazed trails of Connecticut, are natural miracles, which will enthrall the most blasé. The only requirement is that one go afoot slowly, with curiosity and a willingness to patiently watch and wonder. At first one must learn the art of seeing, not just looking.

A few of the most common insects are spiders, ants, wasps, bumblebees, ladybugs, and dragonflies; each has a story to tell. The spider constructing her expertly engineered web; the carpenter ants herding and milking their domesticated cows, the aphids; and the tiny spittlebug hiding safely in her white bubbly foam nest in the grass are all fair game to the observant eye.

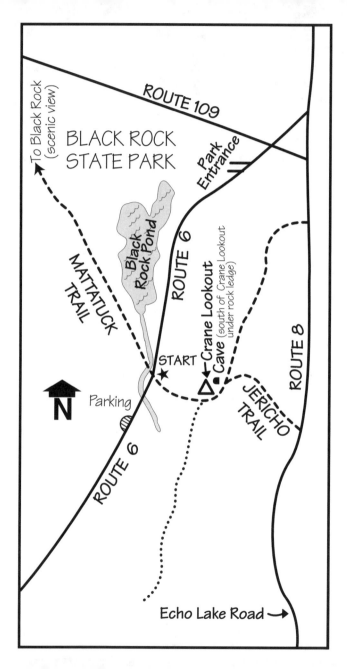

18

Leatherman Cave

Thomaston

An uphill walk over rocky cliffs with scenic outlooks. You can scramble down a rock incline to discover a rock cave, which once sheltered a Connecticut legend. This walk involves a climbing and some bare, flat-rock exposures. **Caution:** *Use care (especially with children or inexperienced hikers) when near cliff edges and when descending to the cave—it's rocky with very steep drops!*

The Connecticut legend of the Old Leatherman can trace its unlikely roots back to the bankruptcy of a small leather business in France and the resulting broken betrothal.

The man who became known as the Old Leatherman was first reported in Connecticut in 1862. Thereafter he roamed the state in a circuit, always in a clockwise direction, between the Connecticut and Hudson rivers. It is claimed that he made the trip winter and summer,

TRAIL TIPS

No facilities. Parking is off the shoulder of the road near trail crossing; use caution when crossing to the trail. Binoculars are a good addition to this walk as views from the rock top are expansive. Watertown has convenience stores and food spots.

arriving at the same places every thirty-four days.

Although the Leatherman roamed back and forth across Connecticut for twenty-seven years, very little is known about him. Only near the close of his life were bits of his story learned. His name was Jules Bourglay; he was born near Lyons, France. He worked for his prospective father-in-law, who owned a prosperous leather business. The young man ruined the business by miscalculating the market and was then jilted by his sweetheart. These losses affected him mentally, and he became an eccentric wanderer. He left France and came to America.

He wore leather clothing from head to toe. His hat, coat, vest, trousers, and shoes were made of pieces of hide crudely laced together. It is estimated that his attire weighed more than sixty pounds, not including two large leather bags in which he carried all his other possessions. One anecdote states that he wore these things as a penance and a constant reminder of his misfortunes.

He begged by gestures, never speaking but expressing thanks for food and tobacco with grunts. His overnight stopping place was in one of many caves along his route. He could not be persuaded to sleep in a house or barn. All his sleeping, even his last, was in a cave. He was found dead near Ossining, New York, in a cave.

If all the caves in which the Leatherman is reported to have slept had a sign reading LEATHERMAN SLEPT HERE, these surely would outnumber Washington's sleeping places in Connecticut. An interesting account of his travels and life can be found inside *The Romantic Legend of Jules Bourglay: The Old Leatherman*, by Foster Macy Johnson (Bayberry Hill Press). The tale makes for interesting reading before or after the hike, and especially to children or those who love local lore.

All that remains of the famous wanderer is a leather mitten and a pouch—both preserved by the Connecticut

Historical Society in Hartford. Sadly his jacket and pants, along with the odd ten-pound shoe, acquired by the Eden Museum in New York, were destroyed in a fire.

One of the numerous Leatherman caves in the state is located on the Mattatuck Trail in a segment of state forest in Watertown. To reach this cave, follow road map routes to the intersection of Route 109 with Route 6 in the town of Thomaston. Drive southwest on Route 6 for 1 mile, passing Black Rock State Park at .5 mile, to the Mattatuck Trail crossing, indicated by an oval blue-and-white trail sign and by blue-blazed trees.

Park your car well off the road, which can get busy. Use caution when crossing to the trail, and follow the blazed trail in an easterly direction, uphill over glittering mica-filled rocks, to a 650-foot-high overlook with fine views. The trail dips down from this lookout, and then the ascent to the top of Crane Lookout begins. The crest is reached at approximately .9 mile from your car. Crane Lookout presents magnificent views in every direction.

Note the dull red garnets (ranging from dots of color to nuggets) in the rocks underfoot, as well as snowball-like blobs of quartz, ranging in hues from almost pure white to those with an orangish cast.

At the base of Crane Lookout, south side, is Leatherman Cave, a most unusual and interesting geological formation, which is also known as Rock House.

IN THE AREA

Nearby Black Rock State Park is perfect for a picnic and an after-walk swim (in season). Walk 19, Black Rock, starts at the park.

While descending the trail, which is more of a side path off the main blue-blazed trail, note the leathery frills of rock tripe (a type of lichen) that adorn many of the south faces of rock. The trail to the cave is well traveled; use care as there are some steep drops. Spend some quiet time investigating the area and try to imagine the life this silent man led.

Then backtrack uphill to the blue-blazed trail and follow it as it dips and climbs onward to its eventual descent to a level forest and meadow area. An unmarked dirt path intersects the Mattatuck Trail before its intersection with Jericho Trail, a side trail leading south to Frost Bridge. You may wish to explore a short distance in this area before returning to your car.

19

Black Rock

Watertown

A steady and sometimes strenuous walk up a steep trail to Black Rock ledges, where there are scenic views of the area. Not the easiest walk, this isn't for everyone. Features include boulders and washed-out areas on the trail.

Black Rock is not black, nor is it just a rock, but a hike to it can provide a worthwhile outlook over Naugatuck Valley and the state park below.

Black Rock State Park in Watertown has every element of an ideal nature preserve. In the rolling hills of the state's western highlands, it includes a stretch of the Mattatuck Trail, as well as Black Rock Pond, Purgatory Brook, and steep ledges covered with pine, hemlock, and oak. The 439-acre park was given to the people of Connecticut in 1926 through the efforts of a far-sighted citizens' conservation group. As with many other state parks, development of access roads and other facilities came about through the efforts of the many young men involved in the Civilian Conservation Corps (CCC), one of the economic recovery programs during the Great Depression. The CCCers are gone now, but evidence of their hard work remains for all to enjoy.

The state park is located 2 miles west of Thomaston on Route 6.

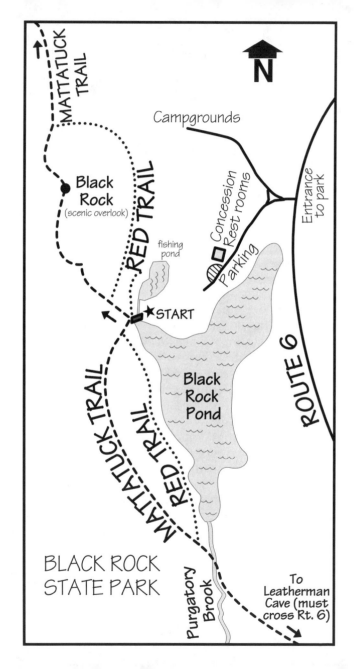

N

MATTATUCK TRAIL

Campgrounds

Entrance to park

Black Rock
(scenic overlook)

RED TRAIL

Concession
Rest rooms

fishing pond

Parking

★ START

MATTATUCK TRAIL

RED TRAIL

Black Rock Pond

ROUTE 6

BLACK ROCK
STATE PARK

Purgatory Brook

To Leatherman Cave (must cross Rt. 6)

It is said that an early user of what are now park trails was King Philip, an Indian chief who pursued colonial farmers in an attempt to discourage settlement. The stone points and implements of Connecticut's first residents are reportedly still found in the park, and looking for them on a hike can provoke interest from young members of your crew.

As the Mattatuck Trail passes through the park, it skirts the shore of Black Rock Pond. To start a walk to Black Rock, enter the park (fee charged Memorial Day to Labor Day) and park in the lot nearest the pond. The pond has a nice sandy beach with swimming area and a seasonal concession stand. Scan the mountain to find "Black Rock," a lone outcropping of stone high above the lot.

Black Rock is not actually "black rock" but a combination of minerals that include quartz and mica. Early settlers in the valley were granted rights by Native Americans around 1657 to mine graphite, a dark colored rock—hence its name.

To start your journey to the top from the parking lot, cross a picturesque trestle bridge that spans the outflow of the pond and a small dam. Bear left after the bridge. (The trail that leads to a campground goes straight ahead from the bridge.) Soon you will cross a small wooden footbridge (marshy in wet seasons) and see blue blazes. A red-blazed trail veers off to the right and provides an alternate (longer) route to the top. Follow the blue-blazed trail and ascend through shaded glades, passing rocky outcrops. It is a sometimes stiff climb uphill over smooth rocks and stepped ledges. Take a break to enjoy the serenity of the woods, then ascend to Black Rock itself, a high spot providing a wonderful view of the valley, the park, and the pond far below.

The distance from the pond to the rock is less than a mile. You may retrace your steps to your starting point or continue ahead, turning right onto a red-marked trail to make a somewhat longer loop back. Alternatively you may continue northward on the blue-blazed Mattatuck Trail to an abandoned road, less than a mile from Black Rock, that marks the end of the Mattatuck State Forest. You can also follow the trail south from the park, into other areas of the forest.

AN OPEN SPACE FOR EVERY PUBLIC SCHOOL

"Every public school in America should have a green open space adjacent to it as an outdoor classroom in which boys and girls can study living nature," said Dr. Matthew Brennan more than twenty years ago when he addressed a group of Connecticut conservationists as director of the Washington, D.C.–based Pinchot Institute for Conservation. Brennan stressed that youngsters and adults alike need places and programs where they can begin to understand and appreciate the environment.

Fortunately Connecticut conservationists have been aware for many years of not only the need to inform and educate the public but also the need to provide open space where adults, as well as children, may come closer to nature. For such a small area, Connecticut is richly endowed with state parks, state forests, nature centers, and the Connecticut Blue Trail System, all within reach of every resident.

IN THE AREA

Camping at the park or at a nearby campground allows the option of staying over and walking several of the trails in the area.

Great stands of evergreen hemlock, along with white birch and ruffle-barked silver birch trees, can be found on this hike. Children may enjoy collecting the tiny cones of the hemlock trees. Should you hike during the summer, a cool dip in the pond is a perfect ending to a day at the park.

Note: Walk 18, Leatherman Cave, starts nearby.

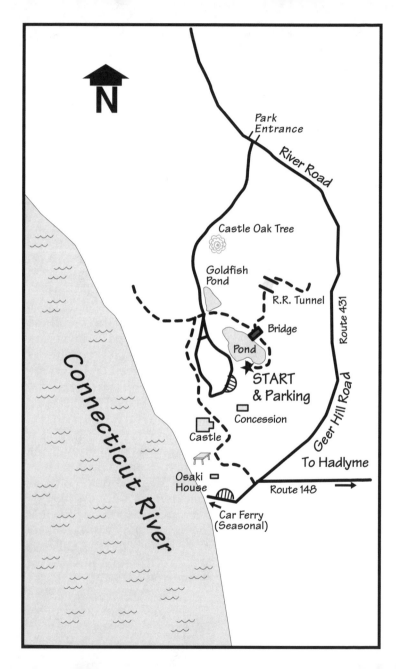

Gillette Castle

East Haddam

A walk featuring a one-of-a-kind fieldstone castle perched high above the Connecticut River. Discoveries along the trail will include an abandoned train tunnel, an odd wooden trestle, decorative bridges, and a goldfish pond.

On the east bank of the Connecticut River is a chain of hills called the Seven Sisters. The most southern of these, the Seventh Sister, rises in the townships of Lyme and East Haddam. It straddles the Middlesex–New London county line, and from its crest one looks down upon the Chester–Hadlyme ferry slip to the south.

Atop this outstanding hill, William Hooker Gillette, famed for his stage portrayal of Sherlock Holmes, built (1914–19) a twenty-four-room, sprawling, towering medieval-like castle of fieldstone. It was Gillette's semi-retirement home until his death in 1937.

THE COMPOST HEAP OF LIFE: ONE BIG CYCLE

From year to year as we revisit forest areas, it may appear at first glance that nothing has changed. The forest seems to have a calm stability, a harmony, a feeling of something eternal. Yet there is constant change. The forest floor is covered with the litter and debris of fallen plant and animal life that is constantly under attack by such organisms as earthworms, springtails, fungi, and bacteria; these decomposers are in turn preyed upon by larger forms of life.

Every living thing develops from elements that once were a part of other living things. Our own bodies are composed of second-hand materials that may have been active ad infinitum in other forms of life. Some of the atoms and cells in our own makeup may have been functioning in the body of a giant dinosaur that once sloshed around in prehistoric swamps.

The castle and grounds were purchased by the state in 1943, and together with additional purchases, they now form the 184-acre Gillette Castle State Park. It attracts thousands of visitors, who may tour the castle and inspect the interior and furnishings, which are approximately as used and left by Mr. Gillette. Some visitors are impressed by the interior decorations of a past era; some are impressed—or depressed—by the exterior architectural style; and perhaps one or two would be described by Mr. Gillette as "a blithering saphead who has no conception of where he is or with what surrounded." The castle is undergoing repairs and renovation; it is expected to be open weekends only for summer 1999 (Memorial Day through Labor Day). Admission is charged to tour the castle when it is open. The park grounds remain open year-round, with miles of trails and stunning overlooks of the Connecticut River, recently selected as one of fourteen National Heritage Rivers by President Clinton.

There are several woodland trails and also walking paths on former railroad beds (along which Mr. Gillette and his guests once traveled in his miniature steam train. The train is being restored and will some day be returned to the park). A concession stand and souvenir shop are open from Memorial Day to Labor Day. Ice cream makes for a cool treat after a walk.

Our small map shows some of the possibilities; the official park map, available from the Department of Environmental Protection or at the park, includes miles of easy walking paths. To reach the entrance to Gillette Castle State Park, drive or take the Chester–Hadlyme ferry to the ferry slip on Route 148, on the east bank of the Connecticut River. The ferry is the second oldest in the state and the first crossing here was in 1769. Be aware that it is seasonal and does not operate year-round. *Note:* When the ferry is not operating, reach the park from East Haddam. There is a small fee to ride the ferry, which takes only minutes to cross the river. While enjoying the boat ride over, you can see the seven undulating hills (Seven Sisters) with the castle perched atop the Seventh Sister.

From the ferry slip follow Route 148 northeast about .2 mile to River Road. Leave Route 148 here, turning left on River Road. An interesting path, marked WALKWAY TO THE CASTLE is located to the left of the road and winds off River Road up to the castle. This is a place to drop off hikers who want to visit the Osaki House (a fancy, wooden structure used as a way point) and later meet up at the castle. If you wish to follow the main trails, follow the signs to the park entrance, about .7 mile. Enter the park and follow service roads to the main parking lot. Note the massive Castle Oak tree at left as you enter the park. The white oak has a girth of 17 feet with a height of 94 feet.

Many intriguing surprises await your discovery within the park grounds. One trail enters the woods from the corner of the main parking lot and encircles a pond. Pollywogs in various stages of development can be seen while looking down from the wooden footbridge located at .25 mile. In season the banjo-like croaks of frogs chime in with a deeper *jug-a-rum*, the signature call of a bullfrog. Trails intersect around the pond; one passes through a now defunct railroad tunnel through a hillside, .5 mile from the start at the parking lot. A pond covered with pink and white lilies contains shimmering schools of goldfish in warmer months. (Save some bread crusts from your trail repast for them.) Bridges, one-of-a-kind trestle and rustic peeled log fencing are features to discover along the wide, well-traveled paths. (Although trails are not blazed, all are easy to follow.)

Cross the main road of the park and head west to trails that lead near the Connecticut River. In winter the patio near the castle is a popular viewing spot for bald eagles that migrate downriver to open waters for feeding. The views of the Connecticut River are breathtaking.

21

Cobalt Mine

East Hampton

For an interesting peek into geology, native minerals, and local lore, this walk takes you to an abandoned mine area with old stone foundations and a small stream. It's a short walk up and down a steep-sided area. Use caution near mine openings.

The Cobalt Mine in the township of East Hampton is of special interest to all who are interested in geology or history.

Cobalt is not blue but silver-white or steel gray and is often found near mica and quartz, as well as tourmaline. A good mineral book with photos can add much enjoyment to a walk in this area, which is a favorite of rockhounds. You will find hardened lumps of what appears to be volcanic rock, although it is actually a type of slag, a waste product that results from the extraction of minerals by heating. Salamanders make their home in the cool glen, and a variety of mushrooms sprout after

TRAIL TIPS

No facilities available. Parking is off the road on dirt pull-off. Cobalt and Middletown offer supplies for the trail. This walk is quite near Walk 22, Meshomasic Forest, and can be combined with it for a day-long outing.

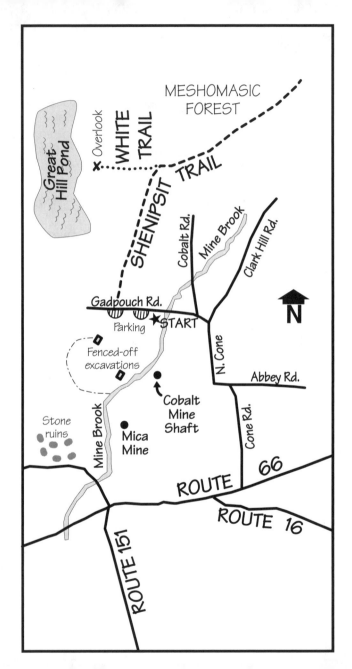

MESHOMASIC FOREST

Great Hill Pond

× Overlook

WHITE TRAIL

SHENIPSIT TRAIL

Cobalt Rd.

Mine Brook

Clark Hill Rd.

N

Gadpouch Rd.

Parking

★ START

Fenced-off excavations

N. Cone

Abbey Rd.

Cobalt Mine Shaft

Cone Rd.

Stone ruins

Mine Brook

Mica Mine

ROUTE 66

ROUTE 16

ROUTE 151

rains. Shelf fungus (it looks like ears) adorns the many fallen trees that criss-cross the ravine.

The mine may be reached from the junction of Route 151 with Route 66 in Cobalt. Drive east on Route 66 for 1.2 miles to Cone Road, on the left. Turn onto Cone Road. In about half a mile, you'll come to Abbey Road. Jog left on Abbey, right on North Cone Road, and then go left on what appears to be Cobalt Road for .10 mile to Gadpouch Road on the left. (You'll have traveled a little more than 1 mile from Route 66.)

Continue on Gadpouch Road a few hundred feet to an open area on the left, between the road and Mine Brook. This, the first of two parking areas, is marked by a line of boulders. Park your car here and walk to the fenced-off, abandoned, cobalt mine excavation. Don't lean on the fencing; it is wobbly and care should be used with young children.

COBALT: IT SOUNDS BLUE BUT ISN'T

Cobalt was used primarily for coloring fine china, especially delftware. "Cobalt" is the Anglicized form of the German word kobold, meaning a goblin or gnome. The German miners considered cobalt a destructive force and a demon in their mines. They named the silver-white metallic element *kobold* because they thought it worthless; and when found in combination with arsenic and sulphur, it was harmful both to their health and the valuable silver ores they were mining.

Directly across Mine Brook, on its south bank, is a former opening to one of the mine shafts. The tunnel is now almost completely choked by cave-ins.

Follow Mine Brook downstream a short distance to old stone foundations—all that remain of the buildings used in the mining operation. It is reported that the mine, which was started in 1792, was never a financial success.

Near the brook and south of the state forest boundary is an abandoned mica mine. Feldspar is also found in the area. Mica, due to its high electrical resistance, is used in electrical equipment. Feldspar is used by industry in manufacturing ceramics, glazes, enamels, and binders.

Time and energy permitting, you can visit another point of interest in the immediate vicinity—Great Hill, 770 feet above sea level (Walk 22). The blue-blazed Shenipsit Trail leads to the crest of Great Hill. This trail starts from the north side of Gadpouch Road, directly across from a second parking area that's a few hundred feet down the road from the first one. (You can walk or drive to it.)

Follow the blue-blazed trail as it ascends quite steeply for .4 mile to a junction with a yellow-blazed trail at the top of the ridge. The Shenipsit Trail turns north; the white-blazed trail leads south to the overlook on Great Hill.

The view from the overlook is spectacular: On a clear day Long Island Sound is plainly visible; Great Hill Pond is more than 400 feet below; the long sweep of the Connecticut River as it flows east and then south through this section of the Connecticut Valley is breathtaking. However, don't bushwhack: Rattlesnakes have been reported in this area.

Note: For a different approach to the Great Hill Overlook, see Walk 22, Meshomasic Forest.

22

Meshomasic Forest
East Hampton

Trek up the stone-studded mountainside to a rocky outlook and views of the Connecticut River and the city of Middletown. Once at the top, the path becomes level.

The Meshomasic Forest is Connecticut's first state forest. It has many attractive features, the Shenipsit Trail being one of them.

The Shenipsit Trail totals some 30 miles in length from Cobalt in the township of East Hampton almost to the Massachusetts state line. A spectacular feature of the trail is Great Hill, located at the trail's southern terminus.

Great Hill is literally and figuratively the high point of Meshomasic State Forest and the Shenipsit Trail. To reach this point, follow the most convenient route to the junction of Routes 66 and 151 in the Cobalt section of East Hampton. Drive east on Route 66 for 1.2 miles to Cone Road, on the left. Turn onto Cone Road and follow it to Abbey Road. Jog left and then right onto North Cone. About a mile from Route 66 you reach a junction with Cobalt and Gadpouch Roads on the left and Clark Hill Road on the right. Follow Clark Hill Road .7 mile to a sign MESHOMASIC STATE FOREST, on the left, next to a dirt service road. Turn onto this road (called Woodchopper Road) and

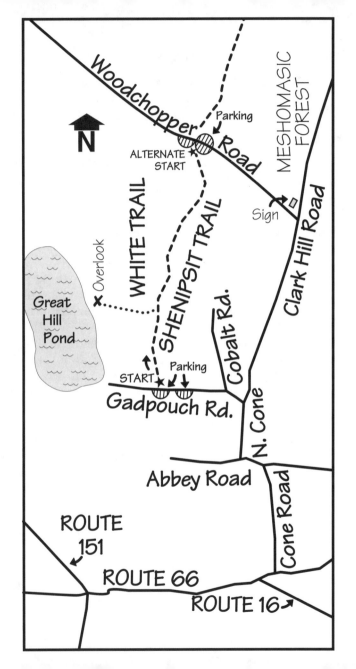

follow it .6 mile to the Shenipsit Trail crossing, indicated by blue-blazed trees.

Park your car and follow the blazed trail south over gentle but rocky ups and downs. At about 1.75 miles the main trail turns left and a white-blazed trail leads several hundred feet to the bald cap of Great Hill. This is the ideal spot to rest and lunch while taking in the exceptional views of Great Hill Pond directly below and the broad sweep of the Connecticut River cradled by the towering hills. However, do not bushwhack: Rattlesnakes have been reported in this area. The Indian name Meshomasic is thought to refer to the many rattlesnakes found in the area.

From this overlook, you can retrace your steps to Woodchopper Road. Or, at the intersection of the white-and-blue trails, you can take the blue trail down to the Cobalt Mine area. Another option is to take two cars and park one at the Cobalt Mine area and the other on Woodchopper Road; walk straight through and drive back to pick up the other vehicle.

Note: Walk 21, Cobalt Mine, is nearby, as is Walk 25, Hurd Park.

TRAIL TIPS

No facilities available. Food and meals can be purchased in nearby Cobalt on Route 66. Bring along water and binoculars—the view from the top is impressive. Wear sturdy boots with ankle protection. For more about the features of this forest, check out a video John LeShane—an area resident and avid outdoorsman—has produced about Meshomasic Forest and its history; it's available at Portland Public Library.

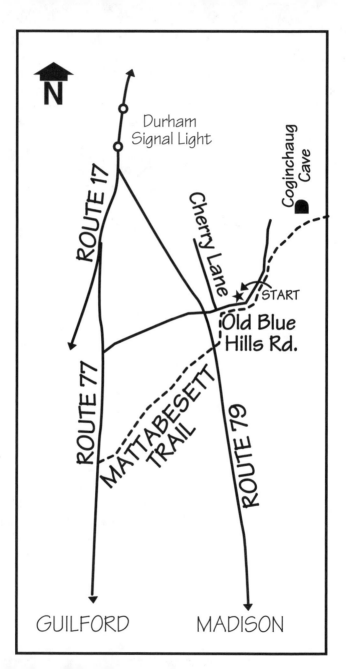

Coginchaug Cave

Durham

A woodlands hike to a cool cave (great on a hot day) over-looking a valley with small streams; some up and down hills and scrambles over rock ledges and a short steep downhill descent to reach the rock ledge cave. This walk is not for the very young and it involves a little climbing.

This woodlands hike to a most fascinating rock cliff called Coginchaug Cave will interest and intrigue you.

Coginchaug Cave is located in the town of Durham on a section of the Mattabesett Trail. Follow Connecticut road map routes to Durham Center. Start from the signal light at the junction of Routes 17 and 79, and drive south on Route 79 for .8 mile to Old Blue Hills Road. Turn left (east) and follow blue blazes on telephone poles and trees to the end of the surfaced road, .7 mile from Route 79. The construction of houses and resulting development have widened the road; park your car off to the side of the road and continue on foot ahead. The blue-blazed trail soon goes off to the right; the trail is well marked as it parallels the road. (Expect changes due to development.) Follow the trail's winding course once in the woods; at .25 mile it bears to the left at a junction. At .5 mile is a stream bed that is dry in summer, with stepping stones for crossing in other seasons. The path now begins to climb more steeply between ledges and over ridges. When fording swampy areas use the convenient stepping stones. Wild turkey and deer frequent this area; by walking quietly it is sometimes possible to catch glimpses of them. Look out for their tracks on the trail.

The cave is approximately .8 mile from the trail entrance, near the road. To reach the cave you must climb a high ridge, under which Coginchaug Cave lies. Leave the ridge and descend a steep slope down the face of the ledge. This part of the trail is a little tricky; care should be taken, especially with young children. Within a few yards the footing eases as the path widens and leads into the cave from the south.

KEEP EYES OPEN FOR WILDLIFE

While it is common to find deer tracks and the evidence of raccoons while on a walk, it is much more common to see small animals. Keep your eyes peeled for wildlife while out walking—evidence of a hidden world is everywhere, from chewed tree limbs to owl pellets (complete with small bones and often a tiny mouse skull) to scat (droppings) left behind on a cleared rock to mark an animal's territory.

—C.B.

Coginchaug Cave is quite impressive. It is a large shelter cave, 30 feet high, 20 feet deep, and extending more than 50 feet along the base of the cliff. It has been reported that Indian artifacts, arrowheads, and tools have been found here. A small brook winds through the valley; piles of boulders make for interesting exploring.

After spending as much time as you desire in the area, return to your car by the same trail. The walk may easily be done in an hour. Should you wish to spend more time at the cave or along the trail, take a lunch and make a day of it. Those who wish to extend themselves a little may do so by following the blue blazes down from the cave, crossing the brook in the valley. Ascend the winding trail through hemlock growth and over huge bald rocks to the top of Blue Hill Lookout. This is a sheer cliff with a deep valley below and a rewarding view over woodlands, fields, meadows, and high ridges to the west. Continue to follow the blazed trail until you feel you've had enough. Remember that at this point you have walked only halfway; don't overdo it. Return along the trail, keeping the blue blazes in sight on your walk back to your car, and then return home both tired and refreshed from an inspiring change of pace.

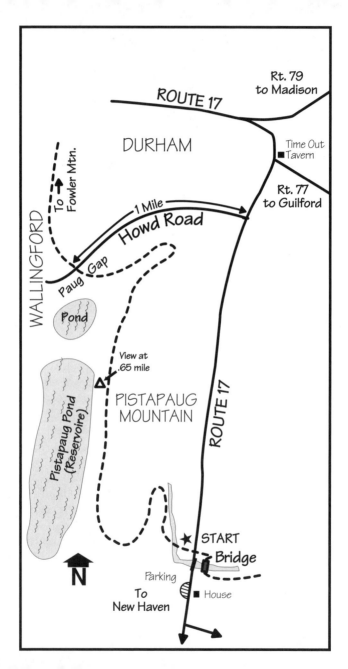

Pistapaug Mountain
Durham

This is a steady walk uphill to traprock outlooks with scenic views. It has a short steep section at the start. Young children may tire easily on the rocky trail.

One of the many beautiful spots along Connecticut's Blue Trail System is Pistapaug Mountain. The mountain is located on the Mattabesett Trail in the town of Durham, west of Route 17.

The trail begins about 3 miles south of the intersection of Routes 17 and 77 and about a mile north of the North Branford/Durham town line.

Park safely off Route 17 and follow blazed trees on the west side of the road. Near the guardrail of a small bridge, the trail enters the woods, crosses a small brook over rocky outcrops, then follows north along the brook for about 100 yards. After bending left, it follows an old woods road a short distance before turning north and then up to the ridge of Pistapaug

TRAIL TIPS

No facilities are available. Parking is off the side of a busy road. Walkers should use care when starting out and at top near the cliff edges. The view of fall foliage and surrounding hills is spectacular. Nearby Durham offers food and refreshments possibilities.

Mountain. The top of the mountain is about 1 mile from where you have parked. Follow the marked trail to the edge of the bluffs, elevation 700 feet, for a fine view of Pistapaug Pond, hundreds of feet below. To the west and south of these openings is a grand view of gently rolling farmland—irregularly shaped fields dotted with houses, barns, and silos. Enjoy the vistas of Whirlwind Hill Road's farmlands in Wallingford and the westward mountains on the horizon.

Having satiated your eyes and senses, you may wish to go on. The trail continues down a steep woods road to Paug Gap, 1.9 miles from your starting point. Here the trail crosses Howd Road, then ascends Fowler Mountain—but you can save that mountain for another day. For now, retrace your steps; follow the trail back over the rocky path to your car.

SIGNATURE FALL TREE COLORS

It's possible to tell plenty about trees just by thinking about crayons. Though nature's palette is much more extensive than the pigments that make up a carton of crayons, by scanning a mountainside, you can pick out trees that go by certain color signatures:

Sugar maples scream orange-yellow, an unforgettable sight especially when seen against a backdrop of lichen-encrusted rock or stone walls. Ashes are muted, purple-reds with an undertone of yellow. Oaks tend to be brown—rich red-browns, tawny gold-browns, and muddy shades. Nut trees are golden yellow. Sumacs are reds, orange, and a hint of green.

—C.B.

Traprock ridges are home to some unusual plant and animal communities. The tops of these ridges are often like meadows rather than deep woodlands. Look for red cedar, chestnut oak, and delicate wildflowers that thrive near sun-warmed rocks. The distinctive traprock cliffs draw the attention of visitors to our state, yet many residents take them for granted.

Today, due to the forethought and effort of many people, the residents of Connecticut enjoy a rich heritage of forest and natural lands in which to roam.

Take your time and appreciate the trail as you traverse it. Observe the growth on the trail and alongside it; learn to identify the trees and plants and you will double your appreciation of these trails.

25

✓ 8/2/2013
w/Janet Peck

Hurd Park

East Hampton

Serene river views, a quiet pond, rushing brook, and wide meadows are part of the attractions on a not-too-difficult walk in Hurd State Park. Water birds and the chance to experience a summer sunset with views across the Connecticut River add to the experience.

A river park with meadows—Hurd State Park in East Hampton was the very first state park site on the Connecticut River. Today its 884 acres are ideal for hiking and picnicking, and it has many secluded spots for those seeking solitude.

The park offers many attractions along with the river and Hurd Brook. There are many hiking trails, including the River Trail and Split Rock Trail. These paths lead through heavily wooded areas; some ascend to high ground where excellent views of the river valley present themselves.

Hurd Park is on the east side of the Connecticut River. The main entrance to the park may be reached from the junction of Hurd Park Road with Route 151. An overhead traffic light 2.5 miles south of Route 66, or 3 miles north of Route 196 on Route 151, marks the junction. From this junction turn south onto Hurd Park Road and follow it .6

mile to the park entrance. (The entrance is closed and gated in winter. There is access to the trails from a small parking lot with map signboard located on the west side of the road right at the overhead traffic light and junction of Route 151 and Hurd Park Road.)

Follow the park road past the power line access road on the left and past a small parking area on the right; continue past Carlson Pond on the right and to a turn-around loop and parking area. Besides the ones shown here, there are additional trails to the river that are accessible from the turnaround loop.

For a not-too-strenuous hike with a lot to offer—Hurd Brook, the Connecticut River, meadows with river views, a steep wooded ravine, and abundant birdlife—choose the River Trail. In just under a mile round-trip, the wide path winds downhill from the parking area. A trail map sign showing a network of trails is located near the turnaround.

The River Trail leads past a steep gorge through which Hurd Brook flows and the woods open up to a wide meadow right beside the river. Picnic here and watch the boats on the river; toward sunset the sight of wild geese flying at treetop level against the backdrop of undulating hills across the river is unforgettable. A variety of wildflowers enjoy the cool damp

TRAIL TIPS

Outhouses are located throughout the park, as are picnic areas. In winter many trails are open to cross-country skiers. Trails are marked with signs denoting the difficulty of the route. Note that the main park entrance is gated during winter; access then is by walking the park road to trails or via the small lot near the intersection of Route 151 and Hurd Park Road. Middletown and Cobalt offer refreshments for the walk. There is an entrance fee from Memorial Day through Labor Day.

conditions at waterside, including jewelweed, milkweed, turtlehead, and dusty purple Joe Pye weed. Sycamore trees with peeling, camouflaged bark tower overhead and the ravine has a few massive trees, including once-mighty hemlocks that have been ravaged by the sapsucking wooly alegid insect pest.

South of the meadow area is a stone slab bridge over Hurd Brook that invites you to sit down and inspect the gurgling waters, or let your legs dangle over the rushing waters. Another meadow to the south adds additional interest and viewpoints. Backtrack to the parking area and choose another trail to walk, or look for frogs, salamanders, and other water critters at the Carlson Pond, near a picnic area located by the turnaround loop of the park road.

Another walk—one of the most impressive in the park— starts from the small parking area on the right side before the turnaround. Park your car, cross the park road, and

IN THE AREA
Walk 21, Cobalt Mine, and Walk 22, Mehomasic Forest, are nearby.

take the yellow-blazed trail uphill. You'll reach a wooden sign pointing to Split Rock, a large fissure in a nearby ledge, to the right, and to White Mountain, about a half-mile walk to the left. This walk offers fine views of the river and its valley.

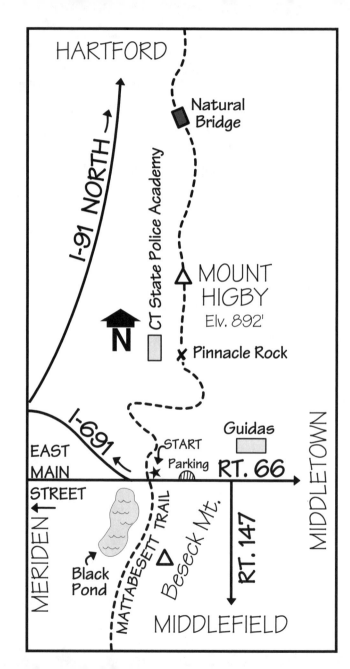

26

Mount Higby
Middlefield

Views! This walk offers the opportunity to scan the Connecticut horizon in all directions, to take in sights such as the Hanging Hills of Meriden, and to possibly see Long Island Sound. Unique geology features such as traprock and ancient lava flows will be underfoot. This walk involves a steady uphill pace over rock to get to the top, so it may not be for everyone, but the views are worth it.

One of the most popular short walks on Connecticut's trail system is to Mount Higby. The view from its crest extends almost 360 degrees from Mount Tom, Massachusetts, to Long Island Sound at New Haven. A portion of the trail runs near the edge of an impressive rocky cliff, from which there are some breathtaking views. Mount Higby is the second highest point in Middlesex County. It may be reached easily from any part of the state.

The mountain is located in the towns of Middlefield and Middletown, north of U.S. Route 66, and close to the eastern boundary of Meriden. To reach the point where the Mattabesett Trail ascends the mountain, follow Connecticut road maps to the junction of Routes U.S. 66 and 147. Starting at this junction, proceed west on U.S. 66 toward Meriden. At .3 mile, Mattabesett crosses the highway. A path begins behind Guida's, an eatery located at the intersection of Routes 66 and 147; this access trail—marked with purple dots on each blue blaze—leads to the main trails through boggy areas.

To start on the main trail, continue to the next highway sign MERIDEN, NEXT 8 EXITS, just before Route 66 becomes I–691. There, on the north side of the highway, an unmarked but visible trail leads to the main trail at .1 mile. Park your car off the traveled portion of the highway and ascend in a northerly direction.

The trail swings west from Route 66 to an old woods road and skirts rock rubble; the path is well worn. Another trail is marked with red and ascends through woods to the ridge. Be sure to follow the blue blazes. At about .4 mile the trail turns right (north), ascending a steep ridge via several switchbacks. (This is not a route recommended for small children; families are advised to use the direct route marked with red up to the peak.) To your left at .5 mile is a scenic view of Black Pond located at the base of Beseck Mountain.

Pinnacle Rock atop Mount Higby is 1 mile from Route 66. From Pinnacle Rock one has the best viewpoint of the surrounding countryside: Hartford and Mount Tom to the north, Meriden toward the west, and a far-reaching view to the south, including Beseck Mountain, with Black Pond at its base. On a clear day Long Island Sound and New Haven are also visible. The Connecticut State Police Academy and a memorial tower can be seen at the base of the mountain, below Pinnacle Rock. Notice that the cedar and chestnut oak trees are stunted and blasted from exposure on the mountain peak. Views of Black Pond and New Dam, as well as East Peak and the lone stone tower of Castle Craig to the west (look for an array of antennae that sprout from the ridge behind the castle), are visible on a clear day.

The bare rock formation on the trail clearly shows how this type of basalt came to be called traprock. The word "trap" is a modification of the Swedish word *trappa*, which means stair. The rock was so named from its general appearance as a set of steps. As you go up and down these stones, notice how they resemble a gigantic staircase. Traprock ridges are a remnant of lava flows that shaped the landscape millions of years ago. The hanging hills you view from atop Mount Higby stand as mute testament to a succession of lava flows.

"NO LEGGERS" MEAN FREEZE AND YIELD

Be careful as you walk and scramble the rocky ridges of Mount Higby. You may want to carry a walking stick and make it a habit to step over loose stone, scanning the ground as you go. Children, especially, should be warned to freeze and yield the right of way to any snakes ("no leggers") they might see—or think they see. Hikers should be respectful of the creatures who make their homes in the woods and ledges of Connecticut.

—*C.B.*

One hundred feet north of the Pinnacle is a large, bare area of basalt, quite flat, on the surface of which glacial grooves are easily distinguishable. Note how the deep scratches line up roughly north to south, the path of the glacier's flow to Long Island Sound. The grooves are the result of rocks and rubble at the bottom of the densely packed ice scouring and scraping the land as the glacier slowly ground southward.

From this point the trail passes through meadow-like

areas with large boulders, then descends to Preston Notch. In colonial days, the old stagecoach road passed through this notch between Middletown and Meriden.

At 1.25 miles is a lightning-blasted cedar tree with three large limbs. The scar left behind by a strike is clearly visible.

Should you wish to extend your walk, you may continue to the northern part of Mount Higby, a stiff climb to its 892-foot elevation. Here is an interesting rock formation called the Natural Bridge. It is indicated by the abbreviation "n.b." on a small marker.

When retracing your steps down the trail, keep the blue blazes in sight, as there are numerous well-worn, unblazed side paths that could easily lead you astray.

IN THE AREA

Walk 31, Castle Craig, and Walk 32, West Peak.

27

Chatfield Trail/
Chatfield Hollow State Park
Killingworth

A walk that offers a ramble over many rocky knobs on a winding trail, or choose to visit the nearby state park for explorations of small caves. The latter walk is geared for families while the first involves some climbing.

A fine woodland walk can be enjoyed on the Chatfield Trail in Killingworth. The trail begins on a woods road on the south side of Route 80, 1.35 miles west of Route 81 and 2.55 miles east of Route 79, and .3 mile west of the entrance to Chatfield Hollow State Park across the road.

The entire Chatfield Trail is about 4.3 miles long, but our walk goes to Champlin Road, an old woods road that crosses the trail less than 2 miles from the start. Park your vehicle well off the road

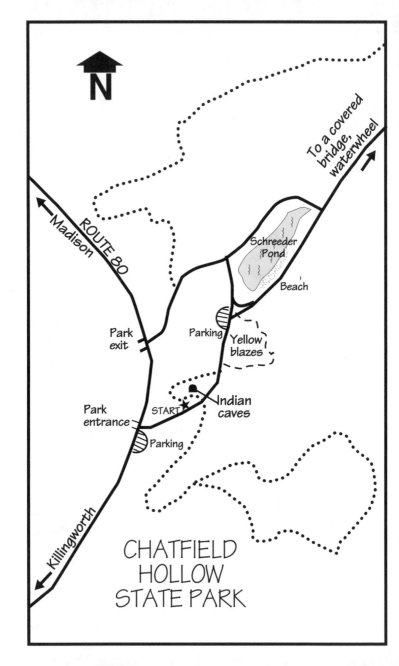

N

Madison

ROUTE 80

To a covered
bridge,
waterwheel

Schreeder
Pond

Beach

Park
exit

Parking

Yellow
blazes

Park
entrance

START

Indian
caves

Parking

Killingworth

CHATFIELD
HOLLOW
STATE PARK

(which can get busy) in the dirt area that holds several vehicles.

The trail begins on a woods road, and enters the woods in about 300 yards. The road itself continues on to Champlin Road and offers a shorter, more direct route. The winding trail, however, is beautiful as it goes up hill and down, along ledges and over a brook.

MUSHROOMS: FUNGUS AMONG US

Most woods trails, depending upon the amount of moisture, are decorated with colorful fungi. You will be fascinated by the normal display of toadstools or mushrooms, surprised by their number, shapes, and vivid coloring. The colors range from pure white to absolute black and a gamut of shades of tan, yellow, red, green, blue, and purple.

There is no visible difference between a toadstool and a mushroom. Both names mean the same thing: a fungus that propagates from a spore instead of a seed, has a common root system of fine threads, and subsists upon dead and living organic matter. One of its chief characteristics is the absence of chlorophyll.

Many of the more than 3,000 varieties of wild mushrooms growing in the Western Hemisphere are found along the blue-blazed trails of Connecticut. Some of the common species are puffball; beefsteak; olavaria, a member of the coral fungus group; jack o'lantern, the underside of which glows at night; and sulphur or chicken, which when fried is a gourmet's delight but is unpopular with conservationists because it often kills the tree on which it grows.

The common mushroom sold in the markets is the meadow mushroom. Oddly enough its closest look-alike is the most deadly of all known poisonous mushrooms, the destroying angel or fly amanita.

There are many rules and hints about how to detect the poisonous from the edible mushrooms, but there are also too many exceptions. So until you become an expert in fungiology, continue to have fun by admiring rather than devouring these pop-ups of nature.

When the main trail turns left onto Champlin Road, retrace your steps back to Route 80, saving the rest of the trail, which continues to River Road, for another day.

You may also want to visit Chatfield Hollow State Park, located on the north side of Route 80, where 7-acre Schreeder Pond, surrounded by pines, is a popular swimming spot in summer. The park has several well-marked hiking trails.

In autumn the main road is gated and access then is on foot; leave your vehicle in the large parking lots located right near Route 80. Follow the main road in; at your left is a jumbled mass of boulders and interesting rock crevices once used by the Indians who gathered here. The trail to the top is easy to follow and leads to rocks, openings, and an outlook across the wooded valley.

28

Seven Falls
Haddam

A beautiful walk on a looping up-and-down path, which takes you over rocky terrain, under forest canopy, and to a brook and numerous small waterfalls. Some easy climbing is involved to navigate the trail across rock outcrops. This day-long walk offers an extensive but quiet ramble.

The Seven Falls segment of the Mattabesett is a magical path that loops and winds along cliffs and rock ledges through woods and gentle valleys. The trail lies between Route 154 and Aircraft Road, and this section is about 1.7 miles long. A roadside park and picnic area is at its Route 154 terminus in Haddam.

Follow the most convenient route to exit 10 of Route 9 in Middletown. Exit from Route 9 to Route 154 and the Aircraft Road intersection. From the intersection, drive south to Freeman Road, then east .8 mile on Freeman Road to a blue-blazed trail crossing. Access from Seven Falls on Route 154 is also possible, though this walk starts at Freeman Road.

Park your car well off the traveled portion of road. Leaving Freeman Road behind, the trail soon forks, with a loop trail coming in at right. The loop trail, marked with blue circles, is a less strenuous and more direct route to Seven Falls. For a rewarding day hike, take the main trail,

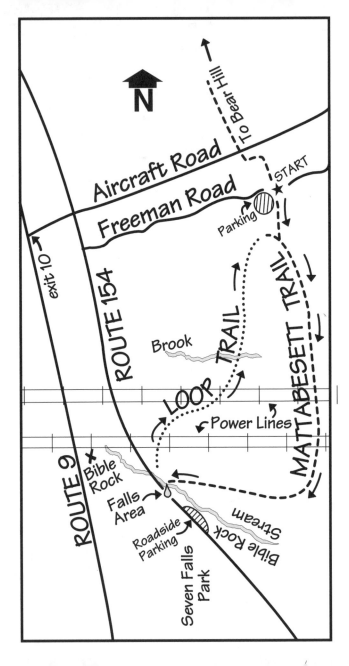

which meanders over rugged terrain, and return via the loop trail for an almost 2.5-mile roundtrip.

Along the route of the main trail are pillows of moss and many glacial erratics—huge boulders that are scattered randomly throughout the woods. Rock cliffs and smoothed ledges make for some interesting climbs and descents. A valley of ferns has resulted from recent logging. The newly cleared area has increased sunlight and the view from atop a rock cliff is breathtaking. The trail winds back and forth across rock and involves a steep descent using hand- and footholds. You will come upon rock shelters and caves, then enjoy a rock "highway" that appears to have been squeezed like thick toothpaste by a giant to make a road—your blazed trail to the falls.

Reaching the power lines on the main trail, you'll descend from rocks to a field area and must look carefully for blue blazes and the path. Enjoy the schist, feldspar (chalky, off-white colored), and glittering mica chips underfoot—rockhounds love this area. After crossing under a second set of lines, keep the blazes in sight as side trails intersect the main trail. At .7 mile from the start is a natural rock dam; blazes take you across the top, but a well-worn path proves that many walkers slide down the rock face to the bottom. At approximately .75 mile is a boulder with a large steel "T" denoting the Haddam and Middletown border. A bit farther on is a gigantic stone wall, as high as a two-story building—worthy of exploration. From the start, it's about one mile to the brook area; use care while crossing on stones.

Bible Rock Brook, with its fascinating falls and pools, is in the area of Seven Falls Park and has a very special appeal. The numerous small falls, potholes, swirling waters, and rocky beaches are a delight. The Bible Rock Brook is named for a rock formation that looks like an open book, hence the name. Bible Rock is located west of the park, across Route 154.

Spend as much time as you like along the Seven Falls area, then head upstream to find the loop trail that leads across a power line clearing, back into woods and rocks, across a feeder stream, and through stone peaks back to the main trail and your car.

We can't all explore outer space, nor does everyone have a desire to do so. It is not even necessary to visit distant places on Earth to see and experience extraordinary sights. One can find exciting adventure, surprising worlds, and apparent miracles right underfoot.

Note: This walk is just south of Walk 29, Bear Hill.

Bear Hill

Middletown

A walk that leads through shaded tunnels of wavy "slicks" of mountain laurel that tower overhead. Highlights to enjoy include interesting rock exposures of quartz and glittery mica under the powerline section of the trail. Some short rocky climbs are fun. This walk is suitable for all ages.

The Mattabessett Trail bears the name that Indians gave to the area that's now Middletown. The trail has three divisions—Eastern, Central, and Northern—that are connected by several miles of paved roads.

The Eastern division, between Route 154 and the Connecticut River, includes the Bear Hill section, a scenic stretch with a high spot, nicknamed the Summit, and a big ledge called the Chinese Wall. To reach this section of the trail, follow the most convenient route to Route 154, Saybrook Road, in Middletown.

Approaching from the north, drive to the junction of

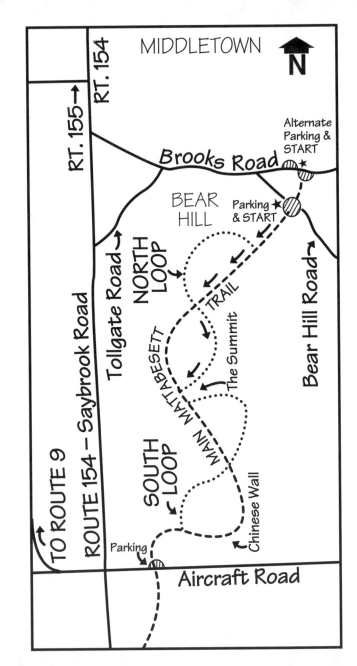

Routes 155 and 154. From the junction follow Route 154 south .2 mile to Brooks Road; turn east onto Brooks Road and follow it .8 mile to the blue-blazed trail.

Approaching from the south, from the intersection of Aircraft Road and Route 154, follow Route 154 north 1.1 miles to Tollgate Road. Turn northeast onto Tollgate Road and follow it .5 mile to Brooks Road. Turn right onto Brooks Road and follow it .6 mile to the blue-blazed trail (which is .15 mile past Bear Hill Road).

Park your car at one of the dirt pull-offs along the road and follow the self-guiding trail south, crossing Bear Hill Road, to the crest of Bear Hill. Look for the blue blazes along the road side or on poles to discover the trail. This segment of the Mattabessett Trail is made up of a main trail and several loops. The main trail is indicated by blue-blazed rectangles; the connecting loop trails are marked with circular blue blazes. Take care to note the blazes and keep to the trail or confusion and backtracking may result. The loops of this trail are marked with blue circles and are less strenuous than the ones marked with a blue rectangle (the main trail). At 2.25 is the Summit, with views to the east.

The primary path is more rewarding and passes over the Chinese Wall, providing scenic overlooks of the Connecticut River south from late fall to early spring. The main trail extends approximately 3.5 miles between Brooks Road and Aircraft Road. At the south end of the trail off Aircraft Road there is evidence of logging, but the trail is well marked and easy to follow.

Portions of the trail wind through mountain laurel "slicks," forest-like areas of this pretty shrub. The curvy laurel branches intertwine to form a dense thicket overhead; the trail passes through areas quite unlike a more typical Connecticut forest of oak, pine, and maple—with only a dash of laurel in the undergrowth.

Smooth outcroppings of twisted and "cooked" (metamorphic/igneous) bedrock can be seen underfoot on the section of the trail that passes under the power lines, and, for a short time, through a meadow. Look for shining, mirror-like mica—an odd mineral that can be peeled off in paper-thin layers. Also found here are such minerals as feldspar, quartz, and schist. Glassy, almost clear quartz can be found as well. A simple guidebook on rocks or minerals can add to your enjoyment of this walk.

Note: This walk is just north of Walk 28, Seven Falls.

Bluff Head
Guilford

A rewarding walk that leads along the very edge of a traprock ridge and to spectacular views. Not advisable for young children as a stiff climb leads right to the brink of steep cliffs.

For a heady and breathtaking climb, Bluff Head, on the Mattabesett Trail in the town of Guilford, is a sure thing.

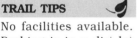

TRAIL TIPS

No facilities available. Parking is in a dirt lot which can get crowded. Durham and Guilford offer many places for a trail lunch or after walk meal. This is not a trail to walk in rain or icy conditions.

A path a mountain goat would love takes you to the very brink of a dizzying view that encompasses Hartford to the north and Long Island Sound to the south; Rhode Island can be glimpsed on a clear day. In the summer it's a cool walk under beech, oak, and maple trees—unlike many other traprock ridges, this trail winds along rock that faces east.

Follow road map routes either to the junction of Routes 17 and 77 in Durham or to the intersection of Routes 77 and 80 in Guilford, whichever is nearer. The Mattabesett Trail leading to Bluff Head crosses Route 77

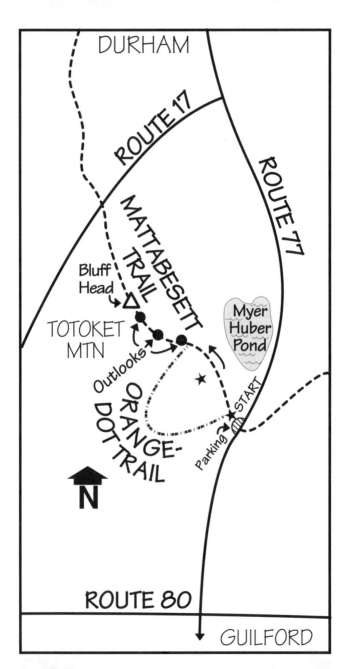

DURHAM

ROUTE 17

ROUTE 77

MATTABESETT TRAIL

Bluff
Head

TOTOKET
MTN

Outlooks

Myer
Huber
Pond

ORANGE-
DOT TRAIL

START

Parking

N

ROUTE 80

GUILFORD

about halfway between Route 17 (Durham) and Route 80 (Guilford). The distance is about 4.3 miles from Route 80 and 4 miles from Route 17.

Turn west off Route 77 onto a dirt road at blue-blazed poles and trees. Park your car off the road at an ample dirt lot near the beginning of the foot trail. (Use caution near the rocks and tree roots.)

Choose one of two routes up to Bluff Head: The blue-blazed trail makes a nearly vertical hike from the very start and presents a stiff climb. In the short distance of 500 feet, the trail rises 190 feet in height. Although the beginning of the trail is unusually precipitous, it is so for only a short distance. After about 550 feet the trail incline lessens and the ascent is easier. Be properly prepared for this walk with suitable shoes; do not try to negotiate the steep ascent with slippery leather soles. The trail can be treacherous, particularly when coming down.

Choose the orange-dot trail, on the left, for a less steep route that rejoins the main trail on the ridge. The orange-dot trail crosses land held by the Guilford Land Conservation Trust. A steady rain of acorns can be heard at harvest time in late summer as nuts patter down from oaks overhead, looking for a place to sprout and grow.

As the path winds steadily upward, you soon find yourself near the edge of a steep cliff, the first of three outlooks.

At the top of the first rise on the right (east), the cliff makes a sheer fall of several hundred feet to the road below. The second outlook provides a look at heart-shaped Myer Huber Pond, 500 feet below.

Bluff Head is the third lookout and requires an almost vertical hike up loose rock and dirt—use care as this is a steep climb quite near a vertical drop. This portion of the trail is not for young children, though families can hike the orange-dot trail to the first two views quite easily.

Bluff Head is 720 feet above sea level. The views from

the top edge of its cliffs are as awesome as any scene in the state. Long Island Sound far to the south; the fields, distant hills, and the cityscape of Hartford to the north—all invite more than a second look.

Bluff Head is a delightful place to spend an hour or a day. Take a lunch and enjoy it while viewing the far-flung scenes from any of the interesting overlooks on the trail. It is advisable to carry your own water or other liquids for drinking. Columbine, asters, goldenrod, harebells, as well as hickory, oak, beech, and maple trees can be enjoyed along the route in season. Autumn provides a spectacular display from this lookout.

Choose to make the round-trip to your vehicle for a pleasant afternoon outing, or walk north, leaving the edge of the bluff, where the trail changes course from north to west and crosses a high plateau where once stood a forest fire lookout tower. Only the concrete footings remain. In its day the tower was a sky-scraping landmark that could be seen for miles around.

From the lookout tower site the trail heads in a general westerly direction across Totoket Mountain and down to Route 17, intersecting it 3 miles from Route 77.

On your return choose the orange-dot trail for a walk through the woods or use care while descending the blue trail on the last few hundred feet of the trail from Bluff Head; the sliding, slippery shale can cause severe spills. The round-trip to Bluff Head on the orange-dot trail is about 2 miles.

31

Hanging Hills: Castle Craig
Meriden

A walk that features Castle Craig, a round fieldstone tower perched on the brink of Meriden's Hanging Hills. This rewarding trail wanders through woods, across traprock rubble, and to the lip of craggy rock cliffs for horizon-sweeping views. This walk is especially suitable for all ages, as a two-lane road (closed in winter) leads right up to the castle's tower and observation deck. Use common sense when near bare rock cliff edges, especially with children. An alternate very rugged strenuous route is provided.

The Metacomet Trail passes over the Hanging Hills of Meriden, as well as over the striking traprock range running to the Massachusetts state line. The length of the trail in Connecticut is approximately 45 miles; it continues across Massachusetts to Mount Monadnock in New Hampshire.

Metacomet was the name an Indian (also known as King Philip) who held dominion over this area during colonial days. It is alleged that he directed the burning of Simsbury from one of the summits on this trail, which today bears his name.

One of the most interesting features of the Metacomet Trail is found on the section that passes over the east, middle, and west peaks of the Hanging Hills. The peaks

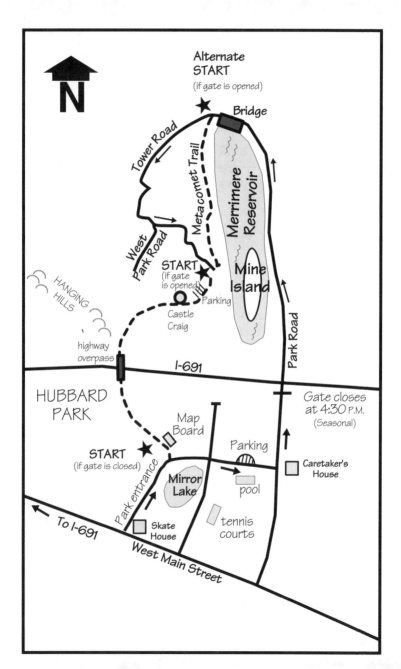

are in Meriden's Hubbard Park and can be reached by car when the park roads are open to vehicles (10:00 A.M. to 4:30 P.M. weather permitting. Closed in winter).

West Peak, with an elevation of 1,024 feet, offers one of the finest views in Connecticut. East Peak is not quite as high. The middle peak has a stone observation tower, Castle Craig, that offers unobstructed views of distant horizons.

TRAIL TIPS

There is one portable toilet near the children's playground at the entrance to the city park. Picnic areas are available in the park and at the parking lot near Castle Craig on the mountain. Refreshments are available in Meriden or Southington, a town just to the west of the park. *Note:* Stay alert for snakes, especially in summer on the white-blazed trail. Walk 32, West Peak, is the same trail, but heads west.

To reach the starting point for this walk, follow road map routes (Route I–691, exit 4, works well) to Hubbard Park, on West Main Street in Meriden.

From West Main turn north into the park entrance just west of Mirror Lake. Follow the one-way park road, which encircles Mirror Lake and picnic areas to a stop sign. Proceed straight past a swimming pool on your right to reach the access road (on your left) to the tower. Note that vehicles must return to the entrance gate for the tower access road by 4:30 P.M. when the fencing is promptly locked. (The park remains ungated and open.)

Note the sheer cliffs with a lone stone tower atop them to your left as you drive the entire length of Merimere Reservoir to a concrete bridge at its north end. The bridge is 1.7 miles from West Main Street. This drive is particularly memorable on a crisp autumn day. Turn left (west), cross the bridge, and follow Tower Road. The first signs of the blue trail are to be seen here on the bridge and trees on the north side of the road. (The blazed trail follows the road for .2 mile from the bridge, at which point it leaves the road and leads south along the west bank of the reservoir.)

Continue to drive along Tower Road from the bridge for 1.4 miles. Turn left and continue .5 mile to a fieldstone tower, Castle Craig, on East Peak. Climb the metal steps to the top of the tower for an amazing view of central Connecticut to Long Island Sound (depending on weather conditions).

Leave your car in the parking area. East of the parking area and a short distance northeast of the tower, the trail is indicated by blue-blazed trees. Follow the trail until it emerges on the very brink of the cliffs, which rise abruptly above Merimere Reservoir. The trail skirts the cliff's edge and gives unrivaled views of the reservoir and the forested Mine Island, which resembles a floating battleship at its southern end.

IN THE AREA

Free summer concerts are a regular feature at the bandshell in Hubbard Park. Mirro Lake is a popular place with families as it is a place to feed ducks and geese. The annual spring Daffodil Festival offers food, music, and children's games.

Or climb the metal steps to the top of the fieldstone tower and enjoy the fine views. The famed landmark "sleeping giant" of Sleeping Giant State Park can be seen quite clearly to the south—try to pick out his features: his head, torso, and legs. Many mountains ring the city of Meriden; looking north it is possible to see the Oz-like towers of Hartford on the horizon.

After viewing the far-flung landscape you may wish to walk the blue-blazed trail leading down from East Peak. This section of the trail skirts the very brink of the cliffs on the west side of Merimere Reservoir. The scenery is breathtaking, especially in autumn. Note the pock-marked stone underfoot—a remnant of the ancient volcanic action that created the Hanging Hills of Meriden. Most of the cliffs are composed of traprock, created when lava flows oozed to the surface and then hardened; erosion has worn away overlying rock and the traprock is now exposed.

You may traverse as much of the trail as you wish and then retrace your steps back to your parked car; or you can follow the trail to its juncture with Tower Road and return by road. It is 1.6 miles to the stone tower via the road. This route is an opportunity to use the two-car method—leave one car at the foot of the path near the reservoir and the other at the summit's parking lot. Hike from the lower road to the castle, then drive back to the end.

Note: Both this walk and Walk 32 are in the same park, as is a 1.2-mile section of the Metacomet Trail connecting East and West Peaks. An alternate path to the peaks is available at Hubbard Park. Enter the park from West Main Street and follow the park road around Mirror Lake to your first left, just as the main road curves to the east. Park near a trail map board and take the white-blazed trail over a walker's bridge that spans I–691 to trails that will lead you up the mountain. Use extreme caution on paths as much of the walk is over loose stone and rubble. The views of the cliffs and narrow gorges are stupendous. There are numerous ledges and small rock shelters hidden in the cliffs.

Meriden has two reported Leatherman caves, used by the legendary traveler who spoke to no one on his circuitous path through Connecticut and New York. For more about the man dressed all in leather, see Walk 18, Leatherman Cave.

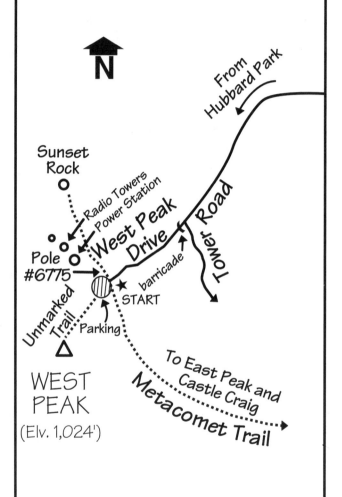

N

From Hubbard Park

Sunset Rock

Radio Towers
Power Station

West Peak Drive

Tower Road

Pole #6775

barricade

★ START

Unmarked Trail

Parking

△

WEST PEAK
(Elv. 1,024')

To East Peak and Castle Craig

Metacomet Trail

Note: Unmarked trail leads off from corner of
parking lot. West Peak Drive is usually barricaded.

32

Hanging Hills: West Peak

Meriden

A short but worthwhile trail that leads past a forest of radio towers and antennas to traprock cliffs and sweeping western panoramic views. Sunsets may be viewed from West Peak but this is only for those walkers who then descend on a challenging trail back to Hubbard Park. (The road to Castle Craig closes at 4:30 P.M. and in winter.) This walk is not for young children or the faint of heart as the craggy, sheer-rock peaks drop off steeply.

The Hanging Hills of Meriden are outstanding landmarks, dominating the scene for miles around, and the views from their peaks are among the finest in the state.

This walk focuses on the West Peak at Hanging Hills; Walk 31 describes a visit to Castle Craig, and there is a 1.2-mile section of the Metacomet Trail that runs from one peak to the other. One of the Metacomet Trail's most spectacular sections lies between West Peak and Sunset Rock, .6 mile northwest. Also worth taking is a short, unmarked trail nearby.

TRAIL TIPS

See notes under Walk 31 Castle Craig. Use extreme care near the cliffs because numerous and almost-hidden narrow ravines provide steep drop-offs.

LEGEND OF THE BLACK DOG OF WEST PEAK

Many old-time hikers in the area can recount the legend peculiar to these ancient rocky hills. Should you see a black dog on your walk, pay heed.

Those who frequent the trails at the Hanging Hills of Meriden tell the tale of a small black dog that makes no sound and leaves no footprints. Walkers who spy the hound once, receive joy; those who see it twice, get sorrow; and to those who glimpse the dog three times—it brings death.

Believe it or not, it's a fun tale to tell as you walk on the peaks.

—C.B.

To reach the West Peak walks, take Route I–691, exit 4, or another convenient route to the entrance of Hubbard Park on West Main Street in Meriden. Take the park entrance just west of Mirror Lake. (See map on page 122.)

When the park road to the summit is open to vehicles (10:00 A.M. to 4:30 P.M., weather permitting), you can travel by car for part of this journey. Follow the park road on the east bank of Merimere Reservoir to the bridge. Here, go left on Tower Road; then veer right onto West Peak Drive where Tower Road goes left to Castle Craig, the stone observation tower.

Note: The road to West Peak is usually blocked even when the park roads are officially open. Park at the Castle Craig parking area and walk the road (about 1 mile) to West Peak.

Next to the entrance to the parking area, at utility pole #6775 on West Peak Drive, the blue-blazed trail enters the woods and heads in a general northerly direction, past a power station at the start of the trail. The main trail follows an interior course with side trails leading to outlook points. About .6 mile from West Peak, the trail reaches Sunset Rock with its exceptional western view.

Take this walk at a leisurely pace and explore all side trails to the left (even those right from the parking lot) as each presents a view that is rarely matched in Connecticut.

From here you can return to the parking lot, walk to its opposite end, and follow an unmarked but obvious trail that offers more wonderful views from West Peak.

THE MIGHTY OAK

Connecticut's official state tree is the white oak. Botanists have given this tree the Latin name *Quercus alba*, meaning white oak, and classify it as a member of the *Fagaceae* (beech) family.

The white oak is an important timber tree, useful and valuable. Its tough, close-grained, durable wood has many uses in general construction, shipbuilding, furniture-making, cooperage, flooring, and so on. The tree's natural range is practically all of the eastern half of the United States. The average white oak attains a height of 80 to 100 feet and a diameter of 2 to 3 feet. It is one of the easiest of oaks to identify because of its distinctive light ashy-gray bark. The full-grown leaves are bright green above and much lighter below, 5 to 9 inches long and 2 to 3 inches broad, with seven or nine deeply cut, finger-like lobes. The white oak's fruit is an acorn, which matures in one year; some oaks require two years to produce fruit. The white oak acorn grows to $\frac{3}{4}$ inch to 1 inch in length, is light brown in color, and is topped with a warty cap.

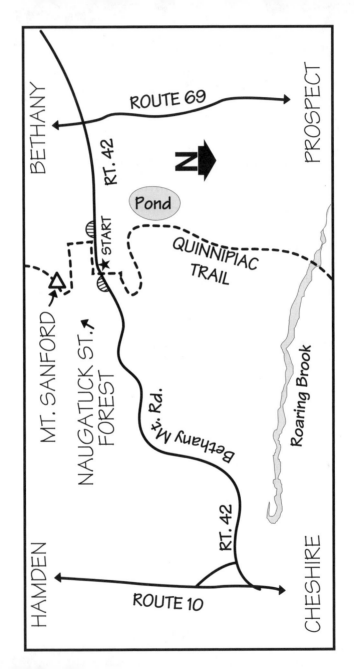

33

Roaring Brook Falls
Cheshire

This steady, uphill walk will take you past a mirror-like pond to a waterfall.

Roaring Brook Falls is in the town of Cheshire, on the northern portion of the Quinnipiac Trail. To reach the blue trail leading to this isolated natural beauty spot, take Route 42, an east–west highway between Cheshire and Bethany. From Route 10 in Cheshire, follow Route 42 west for 2.8 miles to where the blue trail crosses; or from Route 69 in Bethany drive east on Route 42 1.2 miles to where the trail crosses the road. The crossing is indicated by blue blazes, which are easier to see when traveling east on Route 42, since the trail uses a short stretch of the route before re-entering the woods.

Park your car off the traveled portion of the highway.

> **TRAIL TIPS**
>
> No facilities are available. Parking is off the side of a very busy road; use care while crossing it to get to the start of the walk. *Note:* Hunting is allowed in state forests but not on Sunday, wear blaze orange when appropriate. Nearby Cheshire is a good stop for food and refreshments.

Use care; the road can get busy. Take the blue-blazed trail from Bethany Mountain Road (Route 42) to the north. The trail ascends from the road to a rise of 130 feet, or to an elevation of 720 feet above sea level. At this point the trail enters the Naugatuck State Forest and follows the bound-ary line between Cheshire and Prospect. It continues north, passing a quiet pond, skirts a boundary of private property (a horse pasture/house), and over several high ridges with occa-sional lookouts presenting views to the east, the west, and the southern skyline, dominated by towering Sanford Mountain (880 feet). The trail reaches Roaring Brook Falls 1.4 miles from Route 42.

IN THE AREA

The Farmington Canal Greenway, a good sidetrip, is nearby; fol-low Route 42/Bethany Mountain Road east, back to Cheshire.

This is a delightful spot to rest and picnic and enjoy this peaceful wooded area, with its gurgling falls and mur-muring brook. Just above the main falls, the trail goes off to the right, crossing the brook—a trip for another day.

On the Roaring Brook section of the Quinnipiac Trail is a short run of difficult footing, a jumble of rubble and tumbled boulders on a sidehill that should be negotiated with care and proper shoes. The best shoe to wear is ankle-high, with leather uppers and thick composition soles; leather soles are apt to become slippery, especially downhill on leaves.

For a short jaunt into the woods in the opposite direc-tion, take the Quinnipiac Trail west a short distance, past a stone wall, to about .12 mile to enjoy crossing a small brook on a wooden log footbridge. You may continue on the trail or enjoy the brook; it is a pleasant area to spend some time.

34

Sleeping Giant

Hamden

Explore a stone giant with your feet on one of a network of trails across a landmark feature in central Connecticut. The Sleeping Giant State Park offers a walk for all abilities, including an interpretive nature walk.

Climb a chin, walk the elbow, or trek up the head of the giant himself—hikers are sure to feel like Lilliputians while exploring the Sleeping Giant, a forested two-mile traprock ridge that resembles a human figure lying on his back (with his feet to the east and his head to the west). This formation is the centerpiece of Sleeping Giant State Park.

> **TRAIL TIPS**
>
> Facilities in the park include outhouses, picnic areas, and shelters. Bring along a map as trails criss-cross and can be confusing, although all are marked. Should you get tired, take a shorter route; if the day beckons, choose another path.

When English colonists arrived in the area in the 1630s, Quinnipiac Indians were living and hunting on the ridge. It's said that the Quinnipiacs venerated the giant, called Hobbomock. He was reportedly a mischievous spirit who fell into a deep sleep after he tore up and diverted the course of the Connecticut River at

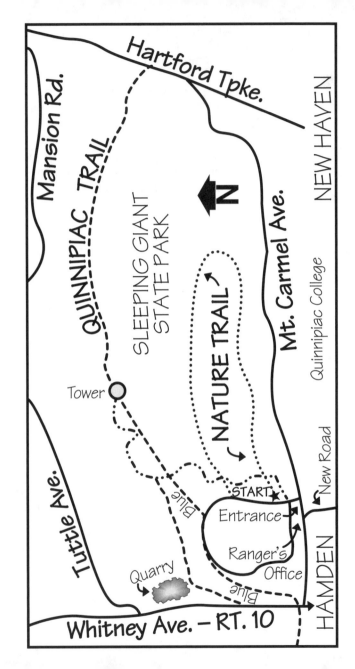

Middletown. Today he sleeps on and his woodsy contours are enjoyed by hikers, picnickers, and nature lovers.

The park is situated mostly in Hamden and includes about 1,400 acres and more than 30 miles of trails, including the Nature Trail. The main entrance to the park is on Mount Carmel Avenue, at approximately .2 mile from Whitney Avenue (Route 10); the ranger's headquarters and picnic areas are here, as well as parking. Many of the major trails start from this point, as does the Nature Trail, which at first follows the wide Tower Trail. All trails are indicated by a particular blaze, either by a color or a round, square, triangular, or diamond-shaped marker. The Nature Trail is indicated by painted green circles with a dark pine tree in the center or by green circles with study-station numbers.

Park your car in the designated area. Near the parking lot is a large wooden sign with a glassed-in map of the park. Also available here (except when supplies run out) are free park map folders and copies of the free booklet, *Self-Guiding Nature Trail in Sleeping Giant State Park*, which is published by the Sleeping Giant Association.

The Nature Trail is an easy, basic education in many things: geology, biology, botany, ecology. The numbered trees and rocks beside the trail are matched with the numbered paragraphs in the guide: trees, ferns, glacial plains, erosion, the difference between traprock and sandstone, and much more.

The entire trail requires about one hour of leisurely walking; it is about 1.5 miles in length. The first part is easy, level walking and can be done by anyone, even small children or elderly persons. The last part of the trail, after the turn near the giant white pine tree, is rougher and steeper. Some may wish to return from here. On its return, the Nature Trail crosses the paved Tower Trail. You can take the Tower Trail back to your car, or continue on the Nature Trail, which at this point follows orange blazes and descends steeply to the parking area.

For a more strenuous trail, take the blue trail from the parking area. It takes you up and around rocks, dropping down to the trail and leading to a quiet walk beside a stream before going uphill to walk over the "elbow." This path leads up a steep trail that flirts with the very edge of a quarry that once threatened the existence of the Giant's head. The approximately 5.1-mile walk is not a trail for the faint of heart or young children. The view of the steep cliffs where excavations once took place, however, are worth the climb. After reaching the top of the head, traverse the Giant's chest and pick a crossover trail that leads back.

Park trails are well marked; be sure to pick up a map and carry it along to avoid confusion or disorientation. Trails are rated for difficulty; the Tower Trail and the Blue Trail are the only two that lead to the stone tower on the Giant's left hip.

MORE ABOUT THE GIANT

The Sleeping Giant Park Association (SGPA), a dedicated and active group, sponsors guided group hikes year-round. This is a good way to get familiar with some of the Giant's lesser-known paths and local lore. If a walk piques your interest, the association has published a book, *Born Among These Hills* by Nancy Davis Sachse. It can be ordered from SGPA, Box 14, 555 New Road, Hamden, CT 06518. Web site: members.xoom.com/sleepinggiant/.

—C.B.

35

York Mountain

Hamden

Scramble up a rocky path to the top of York Mountain for good views of New Haven and Long Island.

Some of the finest panoramic views in the state are to be had from York Mountain in Hamden. Its crest, 680 feet high, is crossed by the Quinnipiac Trail and may be reached by trail from the east by way of Nolan Road, from which the ascent to the mountaintop is fairly steep but only a mile long.

TRAIL TIPS

No facilities are available. Parking is off the road. Use care navigating the stony trail—seeping water on slick rock can make it quite slippery in spots.

To reach the start of this walk, take Route 10 to West Woods Road (just north of the sign for Sleeping Giant State Park at Mount Carmel Avenue). Go west on West Woods to Shepard; go south on Shepard past Nolan (across from the Hamden Public Works Garage). Continue to follow Shepard to a traffic light. Turn right onto West Shepard for .2 mile, then onto Laura Road for .3 mile, and turn right onto Paradise Road, a dead-end.

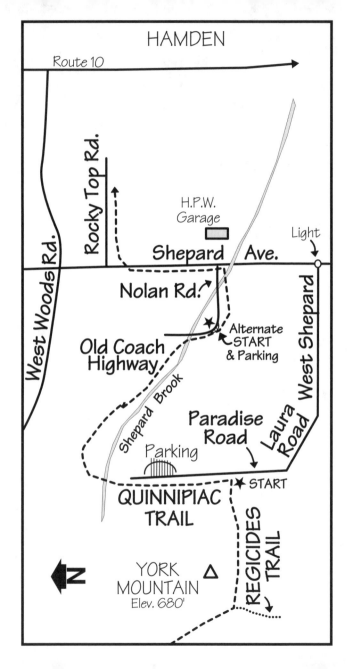

HAWK WATCH

York Mountain is a good outpost from which to observe a natural annual phenomenon—the hawk migration that funnels thousands of these hunting birds through the state in September. Although nature is not always predictable, chances are good that you will see at least a few hawks from early autumn through October. With luck and under optimum conditions, it's probable to see many of these magnificent birds as they wing their way south along invisible (to humans) highways. Birds sometimes just spiral along on thermals (or the sun-warmed air from rock exposures).

At Lighthouse Point in New Haven, some 20,000 hawks are counted each year during their migration south. For details on hawk watches and migrations call the Connecticut Audubon Center at Fairfield (203) 259–6305.

—C.B.

Park your car. Follow the blazes along the road past houses then to the trail (across from utility pole 7278) that leaves the road at a right angle, west, and ascends steeply the east face of York Mountain. The ascent is abrupt—rising some 300 feet in less than half a mile.

IN THE AREA

This walk is near hike 34, Sleeping Giant State Park—a good stop for a picnic. For a delectable treat after the hike, try Wentworth's Ice Cream Shop, located on Route 10 just north of Mount Carmel Avenue. Ice cream sundaes are out of this world. They also have superior coffees and hot chocolate.

To take advantage of an extensive bare rock area where one has unobstructed views of the south and the west, the trails follows the south rim of the mountain about 20 feet below its peak. This outcropping of rock makes the ideal place to rest and lunch while enjoying the fine vistas of the valley below. The green fairway of a golf course far below offers an oasis of open land. Canada geese can sometimes be seen on the course pond.

The top of York Mountain is about 1.5 miles round-trip from the start. Should you wish to extend your walk, you may follow the main trail west to its junction with the Regicides Trail, which descends the steep south side of the mountain to Baldwin Drive. Or continue north onto the Quinnipiac Trail before doubling back.

36

Southford Falls

Southbury

This is a loop trail that offers diverse sights from a scenic gorge with a waterfall and mill ruins to a wooden covered bridge. The trail is a pleasant walk over mostly level ground to a tower lookout past a small pond. Suitable for all ages and abilities.

Connecticut state parks offer natural beauty and hidden historic lore to those observant. Southford Falls State Park is one such example, with 120 acres acquired by the state in 1932 and 1948.

In the days of water power, Southford Falls, with its constant and powerful flow, was the site of several important mills. Water once provided the necessary muscle to turn the wheels of Connecticut's commerce. Perhaps the most successful of all mills at this site was the Diamond Match Company, which recycled old paper and rags to make

TRAIL TIPS

Picnic areas and outhouses are available at the park. Artist Eric Sloane who made his home in Kent, Connecticut, helped advise on the construction of the wooden bridge here. The rocky brook is a magnet for children who will enjoy exploring. Caution should be used near the dam edge.

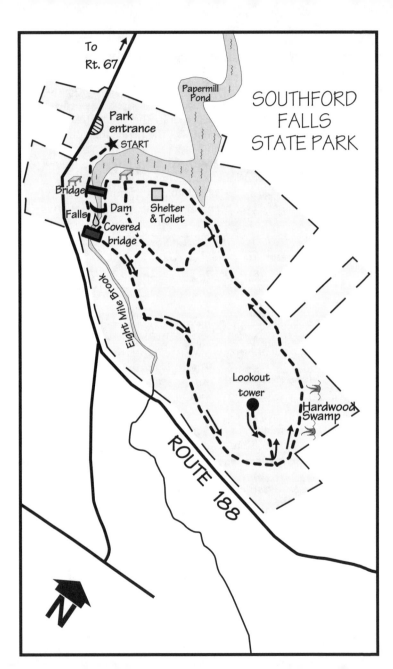

To
Rt. 67

Papermill
Pond

SOUTHFORD
FALLS
STATE PARK

Park
entrance

★ START

Bridge

Falls

Dam

Covered
bridge

Shelter
& Toilet

Eight Mile Brook

Lookout
tower

Hardwood
Swamp

ROUTE 188

N

THE FRICTION MATCH: A POCKET OF FIRE

Early in the nineteenth century, one of the world's most important inventions was conceived. In its way and for that period it was a great step forward, an advance perhaps as beneficial to mankind as the electric switch was in the twentieth century. This world-shaking achievement was the perfecting and manufacturing of the friction match.

The friction match, also known as the lucifer, locofoco, kitchen, wood, or sulphur match, made flint and steel and other crude fire starters obsolete. No animals other than human beings have ever been able to control and maintain fire. Until the invention of the friction match, methods of igniting fire were slow and cumbersome. People therefore tried to keep their fires or its embers glowing, quite often a difficult and frustrating task.

In 1834 Thomas Sanford of Beacon Falls perfected the friction match, which was soon in such demand that Sanford found it necessary to increase production. He moved to Bladen Brook in Woodbridge and built a waterwheel that was too big for the brook to turn. Every penny Sanford had in the world went into the folly of that mammoth waterwheel, and when it failed he was so discouraged that he offered to sell his match "recipe" for ten dollars. The Diamond Match Company later bought the formula and made the wooden match a commercial success.

matchbooks and matchboxes. This once-booming mill was destroyed by fire in 1923.

Today, most of the park's land lies in the township of Oxford, but the entrance is in Southbury. Eight Mile Brook is the boundary line between these two towns in the area of the park. What looks at first like a roadside picnic area is deceiving—the park is extensive.

To reach the entrance to Southford Falls State Park, drive to the junction of Routes 67 and 188 in Southbury. From this junction follow Route 188 southwest .4 mile to the park entrance and picnic area on the east side of the highway. Enter the parking area, leave your car, and prepare to explore the many features of the park on foot. The park trails, worn and obvious, may be followed easily with moderate attention and observation.

The most popular walk is to cross the dam at the south end of Paper Mill Pond to the east bank of Eight Mile Brook, as it falls and cascades swiftly down the deep, rocky ravine. Use care when crossing the boardwalk that has gaps and warped sections near the start of the trail. Continue on the path close the to stream, to the southwest corner of the state park's property. From here you can retrace your steps or continue on to visit the lookout tower and then loop back to the start.

37

Trolley Trail
Branford

This is a short walk through a salt marsh on a boardwalk with views of the ocean, barges, and trains. A paradise for bird watchers, it is suitable for all ages and abilities.

This is a gem of a walk (and a paradise for bird watchers).

Often we complain about the way modern developments mar our natural places. In Branford, however, there's a nice reverse of this—the Stony Creek Trolley Trail between the Pine Orchard and Stony Creek sections of town.

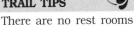

TRAIL TIPS

There are no rest rooms at the trail. Plan on a weekday afternoon and bring a bag lunch—you'll want to linger here. Parking is available near the start of the trail. Caution: Poison ivy grows abundantly along the pathways.

Decades ago, a trolley regularly rattled and clanged along this route. But, of course, that is only a memory now. The main trolley station was once located on what is now Stony Creek Green; there was a ticket office and store there, too. Bus service replaced the trolley around 1928, and nowadays the old roadbed is an easy, inviting trail. The walk offers fine views of salt marshes, tidal creeks, Long Island Sound, and some of

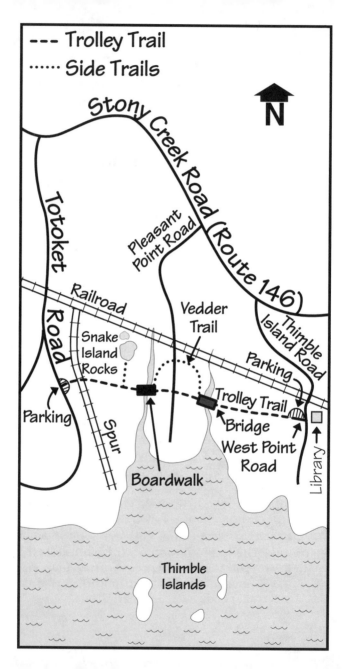

the Thimble Islands. This is a site that draws birdlovers, joggers, and cyclists. Egrets and yellowlegs are among the birds that dine in the marshes, and such plants as wild lavender and seaside roses appear in season.

Youngsters especially enjoy crossing the trail's old trestle bridge near Stony Creek. They also like seeing the small train that travels the spur at the Pine Orchard end, carrying basalt, or traprock, from the Tilcon Connecticut Inc. quarry. (The trainmen usually wave.)

A PIRATE IN CONNECTICUT

Capt'n Kidd, or Captain William Kidd, was one of the most colorful scallywags in history (1645–1701). The pirate is reported to have stashed loot up and down the eastern seaboard, and an actual portion of his treasure was recovered from Gardiner's Island, one of the Thimble Islands. (The islands that make up the Thimbles range from lone rocks to those large enough to host a whole community.)

In 1699 Captain Kidd inscribed his initials and those of his wife in a rock on Pot Island; Money Island is so-called because it was believed Kidd hid his treasure there. There is also a Kidd's Island.

Although Kidd was hanged in 1701, the legend goes that he hid half his plundered loot in various locations on the Thimble Islands. (Which other islands he picked out the hundreds, no one knows—yet.)

—C.B.

The Trolley Trail itself is owned by the town of Branford. Nearby land—which belongs to the Branford Land Trust—includes other trails worth exploring. Near Pine Orchard, a short trail made by the Boy Scouts leads to Snake Island (which is actually a rocky outcrop in the marsh). Farther east there's a white-circle–blazed trail through high granite at the western end of a manmade canyon. This trail heads north of the Trolley Trail, to a high granite outcrop with a monument honoring Jennie Vedder (who donated the land) and great views of the marsh and the Thimbles. It's a loop trail that crosses Pleasant Point Road and returns to the Trolley Trail.

Two roads that head south from Stony Creek Road (Route 146) provide access to the Trolley Trail. On the Pine Orchard side, follow Totoket Road approximately 1 mile from Stony Creek Road to the first road on the left, unmarked except for a land trust sign. Turn in and follow the road a short distance to a parking area. Leave your car and cross the tracks to follow the trail. (NO TRESPASSING signs apply to the nearby Tilcon operations, not to any trails.)

To start from the other end, take Thimble Islands Road off Route 146 and drive about .5 mile to the little shoreside community of Stony Creek. You'll see the Willoughby Wallace Memorial Library on your left. Right across the street from the library is West Point Road, the start of the walk from this direction. Parking is abundant, near a ball field. Follow the narrow path to cross the trestle bridge to the marshes.

A new boardwalk opened in 1998 permits you to walk with dry feet for the entire journey. Strategically placed benches atop the portion that crosses the tidal river allow visitors to observe the ebb and flow of waters, along with leaping fish. Flocks of small fiddler crabs are especially abundant in the mud flats at low tide where they clack and scuttle away in response to the vibrations of your footfalls. Kingfishers and great blue herons can be sighted, and an osprey platform with nest is located in the marsh.

You can spend hours enjoying the marsh, the tang of salty air, and the landscape. The quiet and muted colors are a calming influence. Look for butterflies winging along—a pure delight. The round-trip, including a walk to Snake Island, is less than 2 miles.

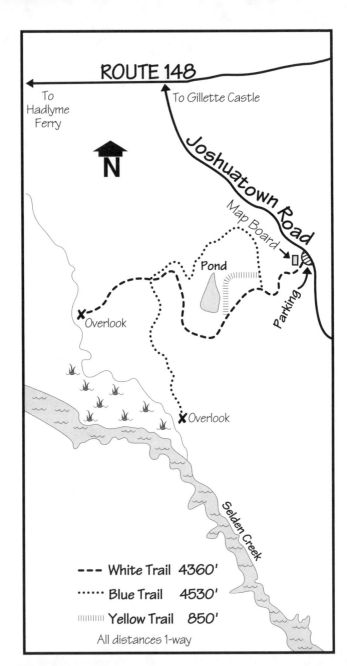

38

Selden Creek Preserve

Lyme

Explore a salt marsh on an easy trail that offers numerous river views, and opportunity to see birds and wildflowers. This walk (except for a low stone wall at the start) is especially accessible for all ages and abilities.

The Selden Creek Preserve in Lyme is one of the most biologically significant sites on the lower Connecticut River. The trails on the preserve are among the loveliest in Connecticut. They are well blazed in white, blue, and yellow, and they are neither long nor difficult.

The wooded preserve, overlooking freshwater marshes, provides vital habitat for many plants, animals, and birds, including songbirds, shorebirds, and rails. It's also a critical site for wintering bald eagles. The trails wend past birches, oaks, maples, and laurel and rhododendron plants, over lichen-covered ledges, and—in the case of the yellow trail—past a little pond (which is sometimes dry by summer's end). Overlooks on the blue and white trails offer fine vistas of Selden Creek, which separates the preserve from Selden Island State Park.

Until 1854 Selden Island was connected to the mainland; in the 1890s—when it was known as Lords Island—it was the site of an important granite-quarrying operation. Today it can be reached only by boat, and the preserve is the sole spot open to the public where "land-lubbers" can view the creek and its marshes. The overlook on the white trail, a high rocky spot, provides an especially dramatic view.

To reach the preserve from the south, take exit 70 off Route I–95 and follow Route 156 north to the Hamburg section of Lyme. About 4.7 miles north of the highway exit, take a left on Old Hamburg Road, which will turn into Joshuatown Road on your left almost immediately. Follow Joshuatown Road approximately 3.5 miles to the preserve, which is on the left. There's a wooden gate, a yellow Nature Conservancy sign, and a small parking area. (It's 1.4 miles north of Mitchell Hill Road, which is on the right.)

From the north, take Route 148 to Joshuatown Road; follow Joshuatown approximately 1.3 miles to the preserve (from this direction, on the right). Route 148 is the road to the popular Chester-Hadlyme Ferry, which runs seasonally. Just to the north of the ferry slip is Gillette Castle State Park (Walk 20).

TRAIL TIPS

No facilities are available. Parking is located near the stone wall, off the road. Since Lyme is the town a tick-borne disease is named for, use precautions to avoid ticks that would like to ride home with you. No dogs (except seeing-eye dogs) are allowed. The drive to the preserve is one of the most scenic in the state. A map board and guest sign-in log are located near the start of the walk in a meadow area.

The preserve is a property of The Nature Conservancy, an international, private, nonprofit organization dedicated to the preservation of plants, animals, and natural communities through the protection of the land and water they need to survive. The Conservancy maintains the largest network of privately held nature sanctuaries in

IN THE AREA 🌿

Gillette Castle State Park, Walk 20, is located nearby. The Connecticut River was designated an American Heritage River in 1998.

the world; its Connecticut chapter protects some 20,000 acres and maintains about fifty local preserves.

In recent decades the Conservancy and local land trusts have worked diligently to preserve natural areas, even as more and more land is developed. The work of these organizations has helped greatly to assure that there are still many beautiful places where wildlife can thrive and where people can savor serenity.

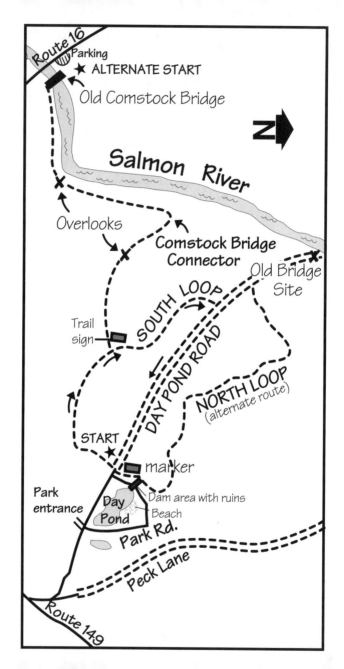

39

Day Pond–Salmon River

Colchester

Ramble along a placid river for stunning views; you can easily spend the entire day at the park. A sandy beach offers swimming in season, and the dam once used by the Day family is fun to explore. This is a good walk for all abilities.

In colonial times a family named Day created a pond to provide water for a sawmill, where they turned chestnut, maple, and oak logs into lumber. By the 1870s horses were hauling wagons across a covered bridge over the nearby Salmon River.

Today people love to visit Day Pond State Park, which is in Colchester, and the bridge, which is a short distance away in neighboring East Hampton.

Fishermen, swimmers, and walkers head for the old Day Pond Road and the Salmon River Trail, which offer an assortment of routes, including one that leads down to the weathered Comstock Bridge, built in the 1870s. In recent times the bridge suffered the indignity of an attack by vandals who senselessly kicked in the old timbers that had weathered the years. Through support from the community, the bridge has been resheathed with new lumber and its underpinnings repaired. A remote camera now monitors the stately structure, which is well worth a stroll to look out over the Salmon River flowing beneath. The route of the old road, over which many horses and wagons have passed in times past, may still be seen. The spectacle of gaudy autumn colors reflected in the waters of the river is stunning, and draws visitors from far and near. Once some sixty covered bridges crossed Connecticut rivers and streams; today, the Comstock is one of only three that remain.

TRAIL TIPS

Picnic spots and outhouses are located in the park. There are no facilities near Comstock Bridge (an optional start), but across the road is Salmon River State Forest, which offers picnic areas and outhouses. Nearby East Hampton has places to pick up trail food.

The Day Pond Park entrance is less than .5 mile from Route 49, 5.5 miles west of Colchester. In the off-season the park may be closed to vehicles, but you can still park along areas of the park road.

Near where the pavement ends is a gate and a granite marker that reads ARNOLD RAVINE WILDERNESS AREA. About 100 yards beyond, the Salmon River Trail crosses Day Pond Road, an old dirt road.

You can hike the old road itself, the trail's North Loop, its South Loop (with its Comstock Bridge connector), or any combination thereof. Each loop section is about 2 miles long; the connector is about 1.5 miles.

The North Loop goes up and down through the woods. The old road (which becomes very rutted and is sometimes very wet) leads to a view of the Salmon River, from the site of an old bridge. After a mile or so the South Loop passes a pipeline easement—an open, rocky stretch. Just beyond the easement, a little wooden sign points left to the Comstock Bridge. (Beyond the sign the regular trail continues back to the park road.)

The connector trail heads through woods and then follows a bank high above the Salmon River, with wonderful views of the sloping bank (often bright with wildflowers), the bubbling river, and the hills beyond.

The trail then descends to the bridge, which hasn't carried traffic for more than sixty years but is still maintained by the Connecticut Department of Transportation. Nobody knows who the original builder was, but he used a trusswork system developed by Ithiel Town, noted bridge builder from Thompson, Connecticut.

It's also possible to drive to the bridge, which is just off Route 16, between Colchester and East Hampton (and is marked by a sign). A parking area is located next to the bridge. Hikers often start here to follow the blue blazes "backwards," toward the park. The trail is on the far side of the bridge, on the left. A ramble along the river's edge can be rewarding; this area is popular with fly-fishing enthusiasts.

BITTERSWEET

Autumn in Connecticut is a natural wonder. Along with screamingly bright colors against the backdrop of old rock walls and green lichens, look for the twining tendrils of bittersweet; their knobbly pods, which are a popular food for birds but poisonous to humans, open to show off scarlet centers surrounded by bright orange leaflets.

The plant uses young trees and undergrowth, such as shrubs, to clamber up into the sunlight. As the tree or shrub grows the vine cuts into the bark, causing bulges and ridges. The resulting swirled wood is sometimes harvested and used for walking sticks.

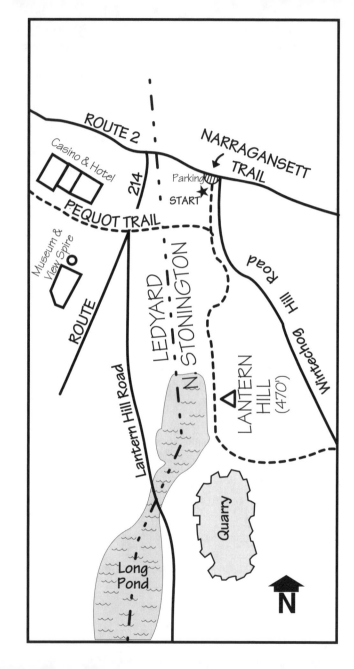

Lantern Hill

North Stonington

An uphill walk through the woods across plenty of exposed rock, with stupendous views of Mashantucket Pequot museum and casino, a defunct silica mine, a cedar swamp, and the ocean. Suitable for families, but probably not for the very young.

For a birds-eye view of the Mashantucket Pequot Tribal Nation, enjoy a woodlands ramble to the crest of Lantern Hill.

The western terminus of the Narragansett Trail is in the town of North Stonington, where it is joined by the Pequot Trail from the west. The Narragansett Trail, part of the Connecticut Blue Trail System, leads to Lantern Hill, then continues northeast for 16 miles to the Connecticut border and Rhode Island.

To reach Lantern Hill segment, follow the most convenient route to the juncture of Route 2 and Route 214, in Ledyard. The junction is near the Ledyard–Stonington boundary line. Go .2 mile beyond the juncture to Wintechog Hill Road.

Lantern Hill is also known as Tar Barrel Hill, due to an incident during the War of 1812.

Barrels of tar were brought to the top of the hill to be used as an early warning system in the event of a British attack from the sea. The tar was to be ignited to blaze a warning if the British were spotted.

That day came on August 11, 1814, when the tar was lit to warn nearby inhabitants of British naval ships massed in the harbor, ready for an assault. The attack never materialized since the locals were so well prepared. The English pounded the coast with cannons to no real effect—the town was well defended and the English set sail.

—C.B.

Turn south onto Wintechog Hill Road and follow blue blazes .2 mile to where the trail leaves the road and enters the woods. Park your car off the road and follow the trail up a fair grade. The trail ascends to Lantern Hill on an old tote road for .4 mile to the point where the Pequot Trail, coming from the right (west) joins up with the Narragansett. Continue south, ascending steeply to the summit, about .7 mile from the start. A trail branches off to the north and leads right over the edge of the rock face; use caution as the drop-off is quite steep.

The crest of Lantern Hill is about 470 feet above sea level, presenting views of a nearby swamp-pond as well as Block Island and Fishers Island, Montauk Point, Norwich, and the distant hills. The blaze of white quartz outcroppings on Lantern Hill can be seen from out at sea, and was used as a landmark for mariners. The hill is also reported to be a place of special meaning to Native Americans. (Saccacus, a Pequot chieftain, is reported to have stood on this summit to look for campfires of hostile tribes.)

Dominating the view from the summit is the Mashantucket Pequot Museum and its viewing spire, along with towering hotels and its casino. The far-reaching views take in woods, lakes, islands, and ocean. The mountain to the west is nearly sliced in half from a now-defunct silica quarry operation. The vein of silica, of which Lantern Hill is composed, is now owned by the Mashantucket Pequot Tribal Nation.

The U.S. Silica Company once operated the quarry, known as the only pure-white silica mine in the east. Twenty-five grades of the white aggregate, sands, and flours were produced from a unique, enormous deposit of white quartz that was drilled, blasted, crushed and kiln-dried, then ground, screened, and air cleaned to be used for buildings, highways, landscaping, and glass. The dictionary defines silica as silicon dioxide appearing as quartz, sand flint, and agate. The word comes from Latin *silex*, meaning flint.

> **IN THE AREA**
>
> Walk 41, Wintechog Hill starts in the same area, farther along Wintechog Hill Road and heads the other direction. The Mashantucket Pequot Museum offers lore about Lantern Hill and a nearby cedar swamp. The marina-harbor area in Norwich (on Route 2, north) is also an interesting stop.

A tremendous lode of silica is massed in this area. Numerous fault lines intersect here. At one time an injection of molten rock flowed through cracks and faults to eventually cool; over eons of time and through erosion, the mass of quartz became exposed and known as Lantern Hill.

Atop the mountain are exposures of spiny knobs of quartz; small glittering crystals may be observed in crevices. Geese and waterfowl can often be seen on the pond far below. Should you wish to extend your walk beyond the summit, follow the trail south and then east, descending through woods and heavy laurel growth to Wintechog Hill Road. The round-trip from your car to this point is slightly more than 2.5 miles.

Wintechog Hill
Ledyard

A woodland walk to a quiet pond alongside stone walls. This walk is suitable for all abilities.

The 16-mile Narragansett Trail starts at the Ledyard–North Stonington boundary line. It follows a northeast course through North Stonington and Voluntown to the Rhode Island border.

Wintechog Hill is on the first leg of the journey, at the western end of the Narragansett Trail. The trail rises and dips as it traverses the entire length of the hill, east and west, a distance of almost 2 miles.

To reach the starting point of this walk, follow road map routes to the junction of Routes 214 and 2 in Ledyard. From this juncture follow

Route 2 east .2 mile to Wintechog Hill Road. Turn southeast onto Wintechog Hill Road and follow it .8 mile to the Narragansett Trail crossing, indicated by the blue-blazed trees on either side of the road.

Park you car and follow the blazed trail east (left) along a well-defined woods road through a lovely tangle of

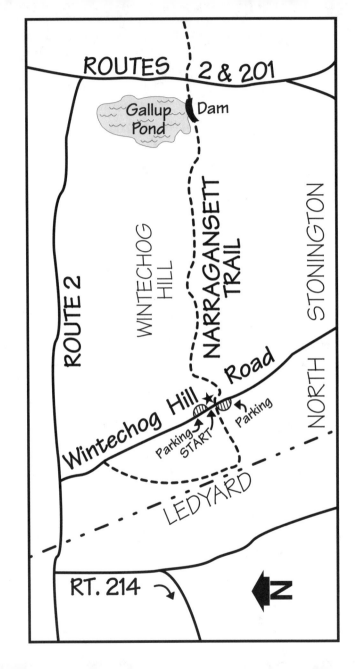

laurel. The trail bears right shortly, then left at the height of the land and follows an old stone wall boundary. Emerging from the woods, the trail descends and follows the south border of a field until it reaches Gallup Pond and combined Routes 2 and 201.

The pond may be crossed on the dam at its south end. The round trip from Wintechog Hill Road to Gallup Pond and back is about 3.6 miles. You may walk all of it or return to your vehicle at any point. This walk may also be reversed, and started at Route 2, passing the pond first,

For an interesting side-trip to learn about the Mashantucket Pequot Tribal Nation, glaciers, and geology of the region, detour to the Mashantucket Pequot Museum. Admission is charged. Walk 40, Lantern Hill, is located nearby.

then on to the woods portion. (Use care as Route 2 is the main road to the casino!)

Or try Walk 40, Lantern Hill, which begins near the same starting point and heads in the opposite direction.

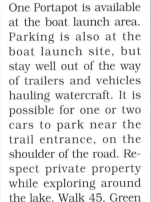

Wyassup Lake

North Stonington

A moderate walk to take in lake, ocean views, plus a Rhode Island vista. There is a pretty sandy and scrub forest area along a lightly-traveled trail.

This section of the Narragansett Trail is about midway in its 16-mile length. To reach it follow the most convenient route to North Stonington Center, just off Route 2. From the village store follow Wyassup Road north for 3.2 miles to a dead-end road on the left. Turn onto Wyassup Lake Road and follow it .7 mile to the boat launch and parking area.

At this point the Narragansett Trail follows the road for a short distance. One-tenth of a mile from the boat-launching area, the trail turns off into a woods road with a metal bar blocking access to vehicles. The wide and sandy trail follows this road for .2

TRAIL TIPS

One Portapot is available at the boat launch area. Parking is also at the boat launch site, but stay well out of the way of trailers and vehicles hauling watercraft. It is possible for one or two cars to park near the trail entrance, on the shoulder of the road. Respect private property while exploring around the lake. Walk 45, Green Falls Pond, is located nearby.

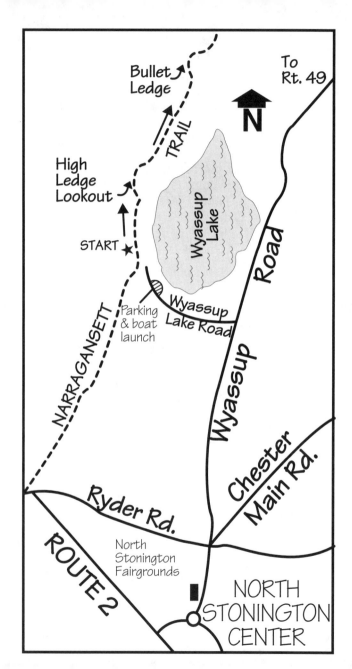

mile, then continues straight for another .7 mile to High Ledge Lookout, with a fine view across Wyassup Lake to Westerly, Rhode Island, and the ocean.

Star-like asters are a common sight along the trail in late summer and autumn. The area is attractive for recreational boating and vacation homes.

If you wish to extend your walk, follow the blazed trail from the lookout for 1.4 miles through hemlock growth to Bullet Ledge, where interesting caves are found on the western side. The viewpoint is reached after a short, steep climb to the summit, about 50 feet off the main trail. (The view from Bullet Ledge is not too impressive, since it is surrounded on all sides by higher hills.) The round-trip (to and from your car from this point) will be approximately 4.5 miles.

SNAKES LIVE IN CONNECTICUT WOODS

While out hiking, it's a good practice to look where you are stepping. Snakes make their homes in the woods and fields of Connecticut, although they are naturally afraid of people and will leave an area if given a chance. Only two poisonous snakes live in the state: copperheads and timber rattlesnakes. Most bites are caused when a snake is stepped on and the animal bites in self defense. Avoid the situation altogether by practicing common sense—especially in spring, when snakes are stretching and sunning after denning-up over winter, and in autumn, when snakes are on the move to find shelter for the approaching winter. Instruct fellow walkers to have healthy respect for the reptiles; the best prevention is education and awareness.

—*C.B.*

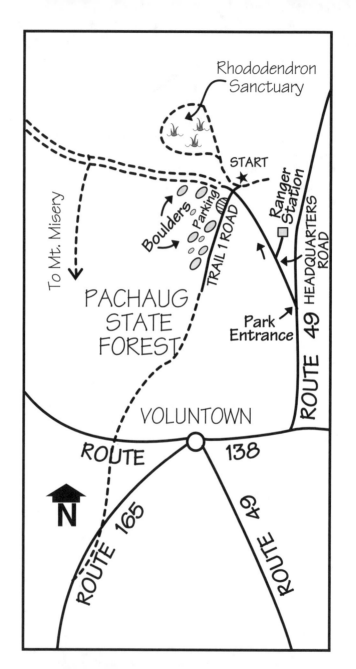

Rhododendron Sanctuary

Voluntown

Travel a boardwalk through swampy tangles of shrubs and wetlands. This walk is easy for all ages and allows views of a virtual explosion of blooms. Birds and insects as well as odd plants can also be seen.

Plan to be in Voluntown between June 15 and July 15, when the flowers of the Rhododendron Sanctuary are in bloom. Of interest year-round, this area is alive with color during that period.

The sanctuary is located in the Mount Misery Cedar Swamp of the Pachaug State Forest in Voluntown. Follow road map routes to Voluntown where Routes 49, 138, and 165 intersect. From the intersection take combined Routes 49, 138, and 165 east about a mile to where Route 49 turns north. Turn onto Route 49 and follow it .7 mile to the entrance of Pachaug State Forest. Follow the park road to a parking area near Mount Misery campsites. Park your vehicle and enter the sanctuary near the wooden sign H. H. CHAPMAN that denotes the area. (To the east of the parking lot is a section of the

---

TRAIL TIPS

Picnic areas and out-houses are available in the state forest.

---

blue-blazed Nehantic Trail that makes a loop through the heart of the sanctuary and returns to the forest road.)

Enter this rhododendron wonderland. The shrub grows profusely and naturally here, flowering in late June and early July. Its woody, fibrous branches reach almost 20 feet in height and are thickly interlaced. A newly installed wooden boardwalk atop a built-up base allows visitors to sample the beauty of this special area, which feels much like a rainforest.

Whether in bloom or not, seeing this evergreen shrub growing wild in Connecticut is a rare phenomenon. Seeing it in peak bloom season is doubly thrilling. Scan the roots and swamp area for a glimpse of salamanders or tiny frogs, especially in springtime. Mosses and ferns mingle with the curved branches of shrubs to create a primeval feel to this walk.

After investigating the walkway via a self-guiding trail, you may wish to rest or picnic at the parking area or in any section of the park. This area is part of 2,000 acres of the Pachaug Forest dedicated on May 21, 1966, as a memorial to the late Professor Herman Haupt Chapman of the Yale School of Forestry for his interest in Connecticut's natural resources.

As unique as the sanctuary may be, Pachaug State Forest has many other unusual plants that should be of interest—bearberry, a trailing evergreen shrub that bears small bright red berries; inkberry, a shrub with leathery evergreen leaves and black berries; sundews, insect-eating bog plants; royal ferns with tall, upright fronds; and the ostrich fern, resembling small ostrich plumes growing in a graceful circle from an erect rootstock.

IN THE AREA

This walk is minutes away from Mount Misery (Walk 44) and can be combined with it for a day outing.

Mount Misery

Voluntown

Don't let the name deter your walk. Mount Misery is a delightful, rewarding, and not too strenuous walk—even in the rain. Fabulous views.

Pachaug State Forest is the largest of the Connecticut state forests and is comprised of about 24,000 acres, most in the towns of Griswold, North Stonington, and Voluntown. The forest has much to offer: hiking, camping, boating, swimming, botany, geology, and bridle paths.

The Pachaug Trail is approximately 30 miles long; its eastern terminus is Beach Pond on the Connecticut–Rhode Island state line, and its west is Pachaug Pond in Griswold. Of the many outstanding features on the trail, perhaps the high spot, literally and figuratively, is Mount Misery.

> **TRAIL TIPS**
>
> Outhouses are located in the state forest. Pack a lunch or you can buy food in Voluntown.

The blue-blazed trail that passes over Mount Misery is the combined Pachaug and Nehantic Trails, joined for about 2.2 miles to follow the same course over the mountain.

Enter Pachaug State Forest from its main entrance on Route 49 in Voluntown, about .7 mile north from the

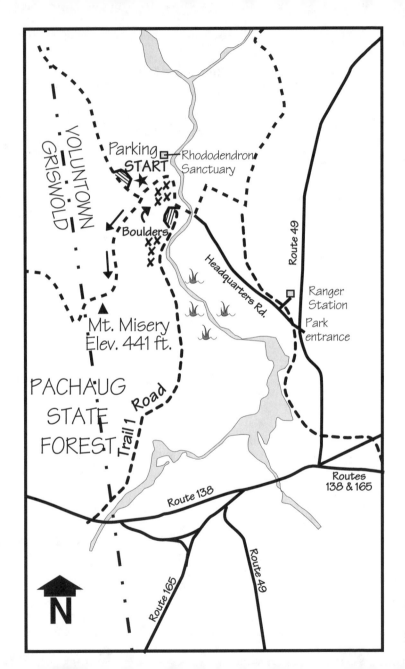

junction of Routes 49, 138, and 165. Detailed trail maps are available at the ranger's station, at the end of the first road to your right upon entering the park.

Continue on the main road to a parking area outlined with boulders. Just past this area is a small pull-off and the start of the walk to Mount Misery. Park your vehicle off the dirt road, cross the road and follow the trail south through woods and across small wooden footbridges. Mount Misery is 441 feet high and part of the trail passes over bald rock for stunning views of the surrounding forest and eastern hills of Connecticut and Rhode Island. The summit is about 1.5 miles from the start.

Depending on the length of the walk you wish to take, you can retrace the trail to the start, or continue on to investigate farther.

Pachaug State Forest has unusual geological and botanical specimens. The great rhododendrons, Atlantic white cedar, and bearberry—all rare plants for Connecticut—will delight botanists. For the geologist are kettle holes in streams and the well-defined ridges known as eskers. Eskers are serpentine ridges of sand and gravel believed to have been formed 20,000 years ago by streams under or in the glacial ice that once covered New England. It is believed that the action of the glaciers is responsible for the botanical and geological oddities found in the area today.

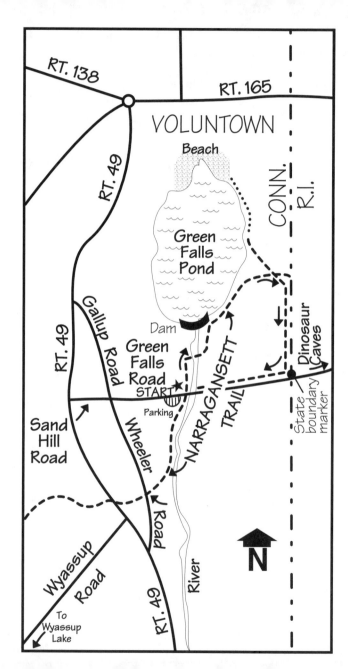

RT. 138

RT. 165

RT. 49

VOLUNTOWN

Beach

RT. 49

Green
Falls
Pond

CONN.

R.I.

Gallup Road

Dam

Green
Falls
Road

START

Parking

Dinosaur
Caves

NARRAGANSETT TRAIL

State
boundary
marker

RT. 49

Sand
Hill
Road

Wheeler   Road

Wyassup   Road

River

To
Wyassup
Lake

N

Green Falls Pond
Voluntown

A wonderland walk that winds through a wooded ravine with a waterfall, through sandy woods and to smooth cliffs and Dinosaur Caves. A highlight of the hike is to stand at the boulder-marker placed on the border between two states—Connecticut and Rhode Island. Suitable for most walkers but be aware that some scrambles and navigation of slippery rocks are involved near the falls and to see the caves. A round-trip journey will easily take most of a day.

This walk has a lot to offer—varied terrain, a waterfall and a pond, caves, and the opportunity to stand on the state border between Connecticut and Rhode Island. Green Falls Pond is in Voluntown on the Narragansett Trail, which terminates at the Connecticut–Rhode Island boundary about 1 mile east of the pond. The rainforest-like ravine, waterfalls, and placid pond make this an area worthy of a day trip—or two.

The section of the trail

TRAIL TIPS

No facilities. Dip your toes (in season) in the pond, while standing on a flat boulder by the side of the water. Use care when climbing the steep ravine and boulders. Ice would make the first part of the journey inadvisable.

leading to Green Falls Pond may be reached from Voluntown's Routes 49, 138, and 165; from this junction follow Route 49 south 4.5 miles to Sand Hill Road. (You will see a small wooden sign prior to this: GREEN FALLS POND on your left as you head south—that road leads to the beach area. For this walk, continue south on Route 49.)

Approaching from the south, follow Route 49 north to Wyassup Road. A church is on the northwest corner. At this point the Narragansett Trail crosses Route 49 and is marked with the familiar blue-and-white oval trail sign. Continue north on Route 49 1.1 miles to Sand Hill Road.

Turn east onto Sand Hill Road and follow it .9 mile to a junction of Gallup Road north, Wheeler Road south, and Green Falls Road east. Follow Green Falls Road east; at about .5 mile the road becomes dirt and stone and there are off-road parking spots to leave your vehicle well off the traveled road. (Use caution on the road as there are washouts and some high spots—go slowly unless your vehicle has good ground clearance.) At approximately .8 mile is the trail crossing, indicated by the blue blazes.

Follow the self-guiding trail north. Descend from the road and reach Green Falls River in a cool glen. Follow the river north and cross on the stepping stones (which pose a problem when the waters are cold and the river is high). Continue to follow the river through a gorgeous ravine that narrows and winds through boulder-peaked crags and hemlock-shrouded passes. The trail clings to the river for .5 mile then reaches the stone dam at Green Falls Pond. The trail continues to the east, involving a scramble up a hill. There is a walkway atop the dam and an overlook of the area. Enjoy the view of water and woods, then follow the blazes along the shoreline, and enter the woods again.

The blue-and-orange and blue-and-red trails (which lead to the beach area) branch off the main trail in this section. Stay alert and keep to the blue-blazed trail. Zig and zag through woods past a lean-to shelter, then to the ruins of a small old mill about 1.5 miles from the pond area. Follow the path east to the very border of the state line. The trail continues south and is blazed blue and yellow; it is a Rhode Island trail.

Traverse boulder outcrops, a bouncy footbridge near cold springs, and reach a massive whale-like, rocky hill. Underneath are the Dinosaur Caves; they are cool even in the summer. (Look for a small sign that points downward to a side path and the caves; this area can get boggy and wet.)

The trail continues south to Green Falls Road. Once on the road take time to examine the stone marker that denotes the Rhode Island–Connecticut stateline—stand with arms outstretched with half a body in one state and the other half in another.

IN THE AREA

Wyassup Lake (Walk 42) is quite near; continue on Route 49 south to Wyassup Road, turn east (right) and follow to Wyassup Lake Road (dead-end).

Follow Green Falls Road west about 1 mile to your parked vehicle. Caution: At least one road branches off south, keep to the main road. The completed loop is about 4 miles long.

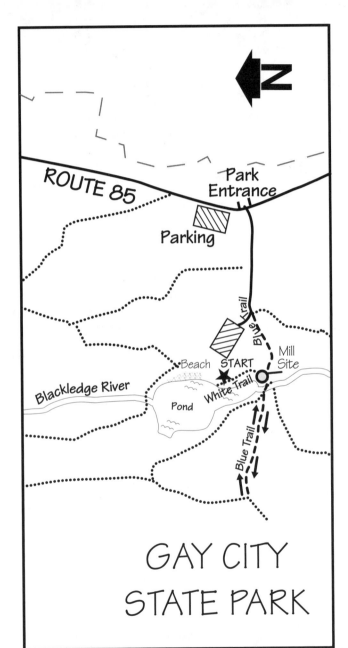

N

ROUTE 85

Park
Entrance

Parking

Blue Trail

Beach

START

Mill
Site

Blackledge River

White Trail

Pond

Blue Trail

GAY CITY
STATE PARK

46

Gay City
Hebron

A pleasant walk in a state park full of hidden history now almost swallowed up by the woods. You can discover a factory and stone ruins or explore a pond with a sandy beach or the banks of a quiet river. Fall is an especially good time to visit as old sugar maples are part of the spectacular foliage display in the park.

Gay City is a real live ghost town, a community that now exists only in the pages of local histories. Once known as Factory Hollow, the name Gay City was stipulated by owners when they turned the land over to the state for use as a state park.

The entrance to Gay City State Park is on the west side of Route 85 in the township of Hebron. It is most easily reached from the junction of Route 94 with Route 85 in Hebron. From the junction follow Route 85 north 1.9 miles to the park entrance. Approaching from the north on Route 85, continue south from the Bolton–Hebron boundary line .7 mile to the park entrance. A variety of blazed trails, ranging from easy to not-too-difficult, course through the park, as well as in the adjoining Meshomasic State Forest.

Enter the park and follow signs to parking lots near the pond. Leave your car; if the ranger is on duty, ask for a free map showing locations of the trails and other features of the area. Maps may also be picked up at the trail display board located by the parking lot near Route 85 (this lot is used in winter when the park is gated to traffic).

A small cemetery located near the entrance to the park marks the approximate spot of the resting places of more than a handful of residents who once lived here. The stones are originals, but they have been moved from time to time and may not actually mark the exact graves.

The area is full of history, even including two ghost tales—one of a peddler who was murdered and his body thrown in a charcoal pit to destroy the evidence, and another of a helper killed outright by his blacksmith overseer when he showed up late for work. Despite its gruesome legends, Gay City is a marvel in the autumn, when the lines of old sugar maples that stand as sentinels at the park entrance become ablaze with flame-colored leaves. The resulting heaps of sweetly scented leaves are a joy to shuffle through on a ramble through the park. A small swimming area and beach are open during summer.

> **TRAIL TIPS**
>
> Outhouses are located throughout the park, as are picnic areas. Glastonbury and Hebron are a short drive away for food and refreshments. Winter-fall-spring parking is at the lot near Route 85. Cross-country skiing is popular in the park. *Note:* Stay alert for passage of horses and their riders on park trails.

A pleasant walk for young or old is the area around the pond, by the Blackledge River, affording a view of old mill ruins. Park trails are well marked and offer the opportunity for a day-long hike or a relaxing afternoon ramble. To find the mill ruins, follow the trail from the beach area (white-blazed) south, paralleling the old aqueduct from the dam, pond, and parking area. Workmen reputedly quit their tasks at one point when this was a thriving community, saying that making water flow uphill was the devil's work. The sluiceway they created can still be seen alongside the trail.

A little bit of background: In 1796 a religious sect led by Elijah Andrus settled in the area that later became known as Gay City. In 1800, after Andrus's departure, John Gay was elected president of the community that soon bore his name. The settlement of Gay City grew and prospered and was almost self-sustaining. At its peak the thriving colony boasted twenty-five families, with the Gay clan in the majority. There were large farms and homes, a sawmill, two grist mills, and a very successful woolen mill. There were also mills that manufactured paper and satinette.

Stone ruins of the paper mill are located east of the trail, looking much like a lost city, draped with wild grapevines and ivy. From time to time buttons are found here in the soil, evidence from the days when ragpickers collected old clothes to make paper—rag paper—at the site. Investigate the waterways and stone foundations, then choose the blue-blazed trail that leads to Birch Mountain Road (about 1.6 miles), or follow the Blackledge River for an interesting gentle walk. Many wildflowers can be found near the water, along with tadpoles, minnows, and abundant bird life. Look for beaver-gnawed trees—most are saplings—along the banks of the river. Old homesites, now only cellar holes, are scattered throughout the woods. Notice wildly sprouting apple trees and overgrown lilacs or gnarled loops of grapevine, planted long ago to grace a yard.

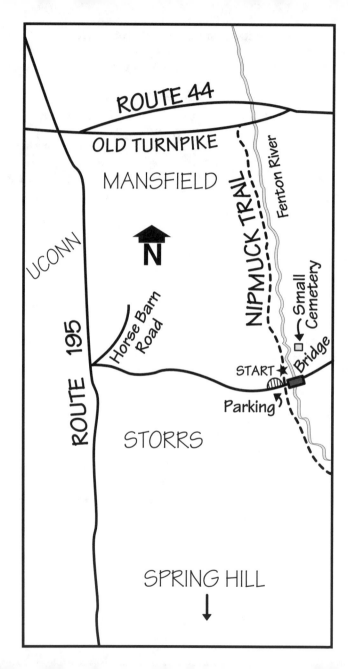

Nipmuck Trail

Mansfield

A serene walk under towering trees that offers ample opportunities for river explorations. Suitable for families; most terrain is level ground. Delightful for naturalists as birds, delicate wildflowers, and insects abound along the water's edge. Watch out for exposed tree roots.

The well-blazed Nipmuck Trail, about 39 miles long, has two sections, totaling almost 14 miles, in Mansfield. A particularly picturesque segment follows the Fenton River and terminates at Old Turnpike (dirt).

This segment of the trail may be reached by following road map routes to Route 195 at Storrs. From Route 195 turn east onto Gurleyville Road and drive 1.4 miles to a small bridge that crosses the Fenton River. The blue-blazed trail crosses Gurleyville Road just west of the bridge. Leave your vehicle at a dirt pull-off located just before the bridge (west.)

Follow the trail in a northwesterly direction, passing some old stone foundations

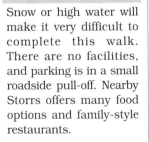

TRAIL TIPS

Snow or high water will make it very difficult to complete this walk. There are no facilities, and parking is in a small roadside pull-off. Nearby Storrs offers many food options and family-style restaurants.

(including a sluiceway once used to harness water power), then through a dense stand of old pines close to the west bank of the river.

At no time does this portion of the Nipmuck Trail reach any appreciable elevation for a distant view; it compensates by remaining close to the river's edge with its contrasting still, passive pools and rushing rapids. The river, which is wide and shallow in summer and early fall, but not after heavy rain or snowmelt, has numerous sandbars and watery pockets to explore. Small fish dart about as water striders ride along the water's surface. At .5 mile is a wooden footbridge that will help the walker if the trail is muddy. Other wooden bridges cross the trail where small feeder streams flow into the Fenton River. The cathedral-like trees and pines make this a cool,

---

SPITTLEBUGS

It is understandable that we would be more preoccupied with the lilting song of a bird or the sight of a squirrel gliding gracefully through the air than with a glob of the spittlebug in the grass beneath our feet.

This white mass of bubbles is found on grasses so frequently that it has earned a multitude of names: bubble villa, froth castle, cuckoo-spit, frog-spit, frog-foam, foam mansion, et cetera. The bubbles are made by the females and young nymphs. The female makes the froth to cover her eggs. The babies, which resemble microscopic frogs, suck plant juices to use for food and to make their froth covering. The bubbles burst and must be constantly replaced.

Gently push the foam aside with a twig, and inside the mass you will see a squat, light green, frog-like insect. Why this insect develops in this frothy mass is anybody's guess. It may be for protection, but the nymph is so small it would take a sharp eye to detect it. In fact, the mass of bubbles with which it surrounds itself may actually give away the presence of a spittlebug to any preying enemy.

shaded walk with layers of leaves and pine needles underfoot, as well as tangles of tree roots. Ferns grow here in abundance; in spring look for the uncurling fronds called fiddleheads, which resemble the curved head of a fiddle.

It is possible to traverse this short section of the trail in less than one hour by striding along, but the trail is so inviting that one is compelled to stop constantly to admire its many features and is apt to spend many pleasant hours here. The round-trip is less than 3 miles, but can easily encompass an afternoon. Pack a lunch and sit quietly near any of the numerous bends of the river and enjoy the calling, chattering, and singing of the birds. You may also have the good fortune of seeing one of the flying squirrels reported in this area.

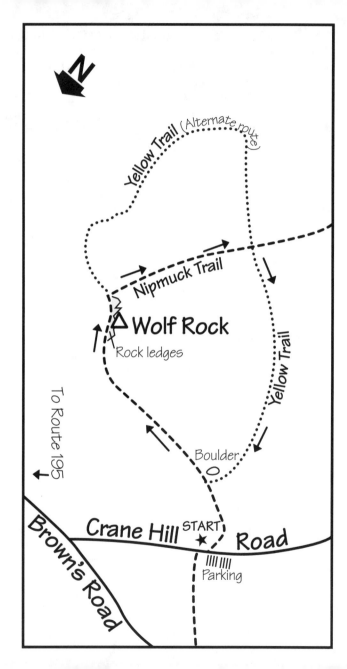

N

Yellow Trail (Alternate route)

Nipmuck Trail

△ Wolf Rock

Rock ledges

To Route 195

Yellow Trail

Boulder

Crane Hill START ★ Road

Brown's Road

Parking

48

Wolf Rock
Mansfield

A woodsy walk with a short stretch along a ledge, which is popular with rock climbers. Along the trail there is an area landmark, Wolf Rock—a glacial erratic boulder. This is a good walk with gentle inclines, not too strenuous.

One segment of the blue-blazed Nipmuck Trail passes Wolf Rock, a huge round glacial boulder perched on the edge of a 40-foot cliff in Mansfield. A connecting yellow-blazed trail makes it possible to do a loop of about 1.5 miles that includes this high rocky spot with its views of woods and fields.

Wolf Rock has long attracted walkers from the nearby University of Connecticut. For even longer, it has figured in local history. Early settlers apparently named the rock after the animal that made its home there (and caused them so much worry). A stroll to the bottom of the stone cliff will allow an examination of the numerous crevices that may have (and perhaps still do!) served as animal (though not wolf) dens.

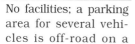

TRAIL TIPS

No facilities; a parking area for several vehicles is off-road on a dirt shoulder.

Today the rock and its surroundings are owned by the Joshua's Tract Conservation and Historic Trust. The trust, established in 1966 to preserve natural resources and areas of historical significance, is named for Joshua, son of the Mohegan Sachem Uncas. In the seventeenth century Joshua bequeathed a tract of land in eastern Connecticut to a group of settlers from Norwich. The trust now looks after more than 1,000 acres of land, many with marked trails, in the Connecticut towns of Mansfield, Ashford, Columbia, Coventry, Lebanon, Franklin, Windham, Scotland, Chaplin, and Hampton. The area covered by these towns is roughly that of the original "Joshua's Tract." In 1969 Wolf Rock and some of the surrounding land became the first acquisition of Joshua's Trust. At one time an iron observation tower stood on the rocky outlook—look carefully and you will find the iron ring bolts left from the tower.

> **IN THE AREA**
>
> Nearby Storrs has a wealth of eateries, including the UConn Dairy Bar for outstanding and generous portions of ice cream (best to visit on a weekend or in summer when school is not in session). See also "In the area," Walk 47, Nipmuck Trail.

To reach Wolf Rock, take Route 195 to Brown's Road (next to a white church) in Mansfield Center. Follow Brown's Road 1 mile to a fork; take the left onto Crane Hill Road. In about .15 mile, you'll see the blue blazes of the Nipmuck Trail crossing. Leave your car in the parking area on the right side of the road; cross to the left (south) side and follow the blue blazes. You'll soon be up on a ridge, and you'll come to a sizable rock less than .25 mile from Crane Hill Road. A yellow-blazed trail is at the right; you'll come back via this trail.

Continue on the trail taking the left path past the rock. The Nipmuck Trail passes through rich woods to the stone oddity Wolf Rock, which sits atop an outlook at approximately .5 mile; the trail then goes downhill almost immediately. Take a side path to the bottom of the rock outcropping. Note that this ledge is popular with rock climbers; should you see brightly hued ropes while on top of the cliff, use caution when approaching the edge so as not to send rubble down on top of the climbers.

After exploring the area, pass a battleship of a rock that looms to the left of the trail, then choose to take either the Nipmuck (blue blazes) back or continue farther on the yellow trail, which goes straight forward for about .1 mile before turning right to go downhill. Continue on this road for a short distance before reaching a right turn, then look for the yellow circles that mark the trail, and head back up the hill to the end of the loop. Follow the blue blazes a short distance to the road and your vehicle.

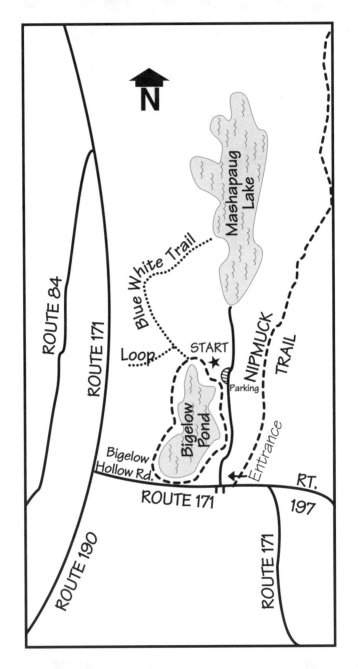

49

Bigelow Hollow

Union

A walk that skirts the edge of a pristine pond (more like a lake) through evergreens, across patches of wetlands, and over boulders. All abilities can enjoy short stretches of this walk or the entire loop around the pond. Caution: *The park abuts remote and extensive woodlands; if you choose another trail to walk, be sure to leave enough daylight to complete the walk and return to your car.*

Most of the 8,058 acres of the Nipmuck State Forest lie in the township of Union. This forest in the northeastern part of Connecticut and close to the Massachusetts border has much to offer, not the least of which is Bigelow Hollow State Park. It is thought that the park area got its name not from a local person named Bigelow but rather from the deep hollow—or "big low"—in which the 18-acre Bigelow Pond is located.

The park offers excellent recreational facilities, including picnicking, boating, fishing, and hiking. To reach the main entrance to Bigelow Hollow State Park, follow the road map routes to Route 171 in Union. The entrance is on the north side of Route 171 and is approximately midway between Route 197 on the east and Route 190 on the west.

Enter the park and follow the service road; park your car in a designated area. Bigelow Pond, which has a trail around it, is entirely within the park. The park also skirts the southern shore of Masha-paug Lake, which got its name from the Nipmuck Indian word for "great pond." A trail is at the southern tip of the lake. Other trails (including the blue-blazed Nipmuck Trail) wend through the park and through adjoining land in the Nipmuck State Forest. Several handicap-access fishing decks have recently been added to the park, which is popular to canoers and kayakers as well.

You may wish to lunch and rest at any of the numerous picnic tables or other spots that may appeal to you, or you may wish to explore the mixed hardwood and evergreen forest. Gnawed tree stumps stand as evidence of the beavers living in the area. Note the lush green carpet of sphagnum moss that grows near the pond's edges and in cool damp spots along the trail. If you are especially observant, a carnivorous plant, the sundew, can also be found here.

The trail encircles the pond and a short stretch parallels Route 171, where the yellow blazes of the pond trail can be seen on the inside of the guard rails. Walk on the inside of the rails, near the water's edge, and then re-enter the woods. Note that icy conditions or packed snow make this route hazardous.

The trail winds along the edge of the water through

picnic spots and populated areas. Footbridges provide dry footing through swampy areas where jewelweed (whose leaves and growth patterns resemble those of its relation, impatiens) can be found. Jewelweed's bright yellow or orange speckled flowers are worth a look, but its plump seed cases are especially entertaining. The football-shaped pods snap and explode on contact—the plant's way of spreading its future offspring far and wide. The plant is also reputed to be an antidote to a brush with poison ivy.

There are numerous trails and loops to explore within the park. Should you desire more information about other features of this popular park, the ranger in charge will be glad to help you, and a detailed park map is available.

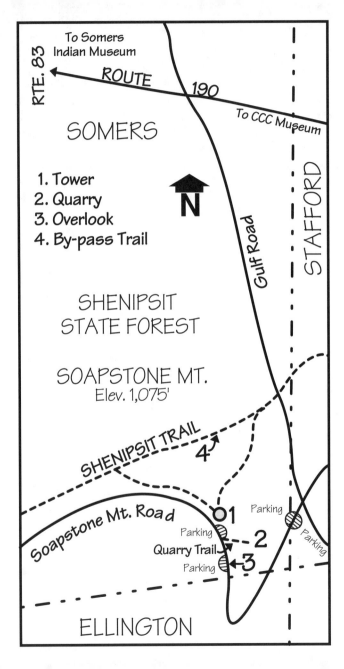

To Somers
Indian Museum

RTE. 83

ROUTE 190

To CCC Museum

SOMERS

STAFFORD

N

1. Tower
2. Quarry
3. Overlook
4. By-pass Trail

Gulf Road

SHENIPSIT
STATE FOREST

SOAPSTONE MT.
Elev. 1,075'

SHENIPSIT TRAIL

4

Soapstone Mt. Road

1

Parking

Parking

Quarry Trail

2

Parking

3

Parking

Parking

ELLINGTON

50

Soapstone Mountain

Somers

Walk to the wooden observation tower that offers great views of a valley landscape. Amazing and popular in fall foliage times, this rewarding walk is for all abilities. Soapstone Mountain elevation is 1,075 feet and views extend over Connecticut to the mountains of New Hampshire and Vermont.

Far-reaching views from a wooden tower, plus easy access via a short drive up the mountain road—that's part of the beauty of Soapstone Mountain.

Soapstone Mountain stands in the southeast corner of the township of Somers, close to where the boundary lines of Ellington, Stafford, and Somers join. The mountain is on the Shenipsit Trail and in the Shenipsit State Forest.

Elevation is 1,075 feet above sea level. At the top are a weather-relay station and a fire tower that offers spectacular views. Soapstone Mountain Road, which is paved, leads up the mountain.

TRAIL TIPS

Outhouses are located near the tower at the top of the mountain, as are picnic spots. Parking is available in a lot near the tower as well. The road leading to the mountain is open year-round during daylight hours, but may be closed by snow.

The least complicated approach to Soapstone Mountain is from the intersection of Gulf Road with Route 190 in the town of Somers. The intersection is 1.2 miles east of Route 83, using Route 190. At the intersection, turn southeast onto Gulf Road and drive just under 2 miles to an entrance to the Shenipsit State Forest. Leave your car in the parking area to proceed on foot, or continue by car and turn west onto Soapstone Mountain Road. It ascends to a sharp hairpin turn before reaching a fine overlook at .8 mile from Gulf Road. Stop at the overlook and take in the distant views to the south and east. Near the top of the mountain is a picnic area with portable rest rooms. Just beyond is the weather-relay station, closed off from the public by a wire fence. From this area, a short trail leads to the wooden fire tower behind the station.

From Soapstone Mountain Road, many connecting trails lead to interesting walks. A trail (just before the hairpin curve as you head up the mountain) leads off the road to an old soapstone quarry, for which the mountain is named.

Soapstone is known as steatite or talc and has a greasy feel to it. Examples of bowls carved from soapstone (perhaps mined from this very mountain) are on display at the Mashantucket Pequot Indian Museum in Mashantucket (Ledyard).

Nathan Hale Trails
Coventry

An outing well-suited for anyone who loves the outdoors and history. This level-ground walk winds through quiet woods and fields, and includes a brief sidetrip to a historic old oak. When combined with a visit to the historic Nathan Hale Homestead, the walk makes a perfect day trip.

Connecticut native Nathan Hale was only twenty-one when he declared "I only regret that I have but one life to lose for my country" and was subsequently hanged for the high crime of treason by the British. There are several sites in the state where Hale taught as a schoolteacher, but this walk takes you near his boyhood home and birthplace.

Captain Nathan Hale is the state's official hero; he was hanged in New York City and his grave remains unknown; most likely it is under the streets of Manhattan.

Traverse quiet forest and perhaps the same ground the young Hale may have explored long before he went to Yale University to become a schoolteacher and then on to serve

> ### TRAIL TIPS
> No facilities available. The trails are not blazed but are easy to follow. Parking is available off-road or near the lot of the homestead. Coventry is the nearest town for supplies and refreshments.

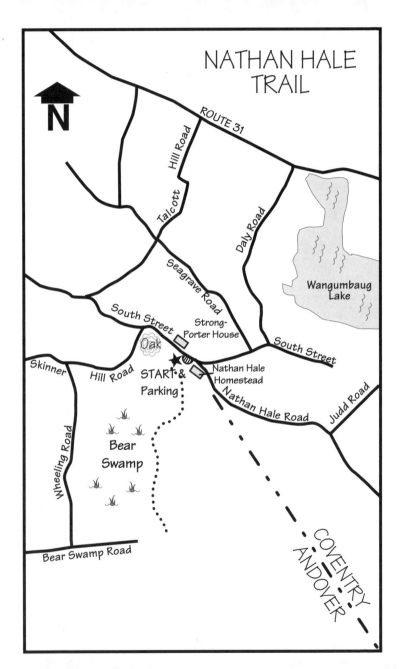

his fledging nation as an undercover agent. This trail is near the 300-acre Nathan Hale State Forest, which surrounds the Nathan Hale Homestead lands.

Follow state routes to Coventry center; take Route 6 southeast from Bolton or Route 44. Follow Cross Street to end and turn right on South Street 1.4 miles to stop sign and fork in the road. Go left .4 mile to the Hale Homestead. Signs directing travelers to the Hale Homestead are numerous. Trails and historic sites lead off South Street.

Park near the trail entrance, .1 mile west of north entrance of the homestead. Limited parking is available at the homestead lot when it is open. (The house-museum makes for a very interesting side trip, especially the stone pyramid tower that marks the resting spot for Thomas Hooker Bones—a horse!)

Enter the path, which wanders through a grove of chestnut trees. In autumn the spiny cases of the chestnut open to reveal their mahogany-colored nuts.

At less than a mile, you can glimpse the pasture and nearby barn of the Hale Homestead through a break in the stone wall. It's quite easy to conjure up Hale and his friends walking and playing along these very paths more than 200 years ago. The house is not actually the one Hale was born in (that one was located near the red building that stands today, but was torn down when the new, and grander home was finished the year Nathan Hale died), but many family artifacts are on display, including Hale's fowling piece—the hunting gun he used as a boy—and his powder horn.

Two small ponds west of the trail are home to frogs and water creatures as well as sphagnum moss and sedges—plants that like damp roots and boggy conditions.

The path is not blazed in any way; stay on the main trail, which leads downhill, past a now-open meadow that has been logged, and on to Bear Swamp. Walk the entire path or any portion of it—the varied terrain and history make this an appealing area.

The grove of maples in front of the Nathan Hale Homestead are called the Holy Grove and consist of sugar maples planted in 1812. The name is due to services held under the trees by a member of the Hale family.

For an interesting short side trip, walk or drive South Street to a spot directly across from the Strong-Porter House, built in 1730. Two stone monuments (one to the chief forester of Connecticut Harry McKusick and the other to the site of the house of Asher Wright, Nathan Hale's boyhood friend and army attendant) flank an old cart path where you may park. Be sure to read the inscription about Asher Wright; it may conjure up a picture of the area as it was long ago. Just a short jaunt down the inviting path is an enormous oak. Perhaps it was standing when Hale and his friends roamed these woods.

Return to your vehicle, or choose another area trail (one leads off the Hale Homestead parking lot), or visit one of the historic sites in the area.

IN THE AREA

The Nathan Hale Homestead is open to the public (mid-May through mid-October), and a barn serves as a gift shop and tour center. Caprilands, a renowned herb farm on Silver Street in Coventry, is a great lunch spot.

w/ Caroline 4/2018

Goodwin State Forest ✓

Hampton

A relaxing, mostly level lakeside walk through woods. Explore a trailside meadow with plenty of bird life and wildflowers in season to enjoy. Most of the terrain is easy to navigate for all ages and abilities.

All the Connecticut Blue Trails, state forests, and state parks may and should be revisited again and again. One cannot cover completely or thoroughly even the smallest area in one short walk. Each return visit will bring to light new and interesting features not discovered or seen on previous walks. Not only do the scenes change and take on a different aspect as the seasons change, but something new is apt to present itself from day to day to those who are consciously observant.

> **TRAIL TIPS**
>
> Outhouses on site year-round. The complete network of trails is posted on an information board near the main, loose-stone parking lot. Bring refreshments or pick them up on your drive to the forest.

This is certainly true of the James L. Goodwin State Forest and Conservation Center in the township of Hampton. The main entrance to the Conservation Center is on the north side of Route 6, approximately 3 miles east of

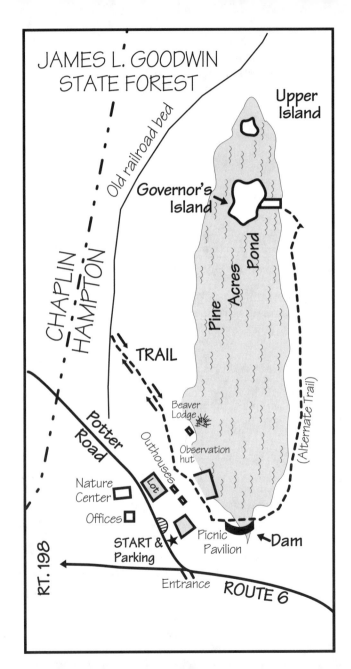

JAMES L. GOODWIN
STATE FOREST

Upper
Island

Old railroad bed

Governor's
Island

Pine Acres Pond

CHAPLIN
HAMPTON

(Alternate Trail)

TRAIL

Beaver
Lodge

Potter
Road

Observation
hut

Outhouses

Nature
Center

Lot

Offices

START &
Parking

Picnic
Pavilion

Dam

RT. 198

Entrance

ROUTE 6

Route 198. Turn onto Potter Road and drive the short distance to the parking area.

The center's offices are in a big white house. A Nature Center is open to the public on Saturdays and for a variety of programs for school groups and the public. Maps and newsletters are available at either building or on the bulletin board near the parking lot. The official park map shows more possibilities for walking than the trail and old railroad bed on our small map.

The property has a great variety of trees and animals. Deer are numerous and beavers are active in the three ponds that have been constructed in the forest. The largest is Pine Acres Pond, about 100 acres in size and open to canoeing and rowing. The Goodwin State Forest was donated to Connecticut by James L. Goodwin, a pioneer in the field of forestry who wanted to help people learn about wildlife and forests.

An open meadow that slopes down to Pine Acres Pond is filled with wildflowers and insect life; in winter the resulting seedpods and egg cases make for some interesting discoveries. A short nature trail winds downhill and interpretive signs along the path enhance the walk. For instance Virginia creeper, called the "muscle plant," can support 2 pounds with its threadlike stems. Other signs provide details about the red maple and milkweed. Butterflies dance above the flowers and hawks soar along the edge of the woods as they hunt for food. A wooden observation deck at the pond allows visitors to gaze out over the water. In summer pond lilies carpet the surface of the water and dragonflies flit along the edges. A large beaver lodge can be seen to the left of the viewing platform. One hike begins at the parking lot, winds to the lake and skirts the edge of the pond.

You can also access this path through a stone wall near the pond's observation platform. Once on the trail, it is a short walk to a small shed, located to the right of the trail near a beaver lodge; sit quietly and look out from the shed's slot-like windows to observe beavers, North America's largest rodent. Evidence of beavers can be seen on the trail: Trees are gnawed halfway through and fresh wood chips litter the ground. Fishing birds, such as the blue heron or snowy egret, may also be glimpsed at water's edge. A sea of ferns marks this area as a wet zone; small bridges and logs will help you avoid covering your shoes in black marsh muck. At about 1 mile the trail heads inland, away from the water. Note the masses of wild grapevine and other climbing plants, and be sure not to touch the hairy-rooted poison ivy vine that clambers up the sides of many of the pine trees.

A wide variety of plant life, from bittersweet vine tangles to shrubs and wildflowers, grows at the edge of the woods where meadow and forest mingle. A round-trip loop back to the parking lot is 2 miles on this trail, an easy walk packed with interesting details. Follow another path south to the dam at Pine Acres Pond and then on to a trail that circuits around Brown Hill Pond for a longer walk. The trails are popular for cross-country skiing.

Nature programs and family nights (campfires, evening walks) are offered at various times throughout the year. Goodwin State Forest abuts the Natchaug State Forest to the north and offers miles of interlaced trails. A large picnic pavilion is located across the road from the Nature Center.

53

Putnam Wolf Den,
Stone Indian Chair
Pomfret

A walk with two destinations—a stone chair natural forma-
tion overlooking a small valley and a cave that brings a
page of the past alive. Depending on which options are cho-
sen this woodsy walk can be for all abilities.

Connecticut is full of hidden history. Somehow stories
about the past are more compelling at the location where
they happened. This hike includes a curious rock formation, the Indian Chair, and a page from the past that illustrates an exploit of the Revolutionary hero Major
General Israel Putnam.

Affectionately called "Old Put," Putnam was beloved by
his men and was the subject of numerous humorous, as
well as serious, anecdotes. Born in 1718 in Massachusetts, Putnam as a young man moved to Pomfret, Connecticut, where he became a prosperous innkeeper and
successful farmer. It is alleged that he answered the call
to join the Continentals at Lexington so hurriedly that he
left his plow halfway down a furrow in the middle of a
field. He served conspicuously at the Battle of Bunker
Hill. Promoted to major general, he commanded the
American forces at the Battle of Long Island. He was the

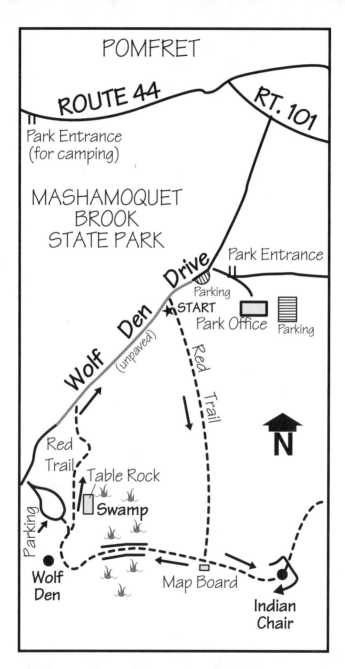

senior major general of the Continental Army and in command of the right wing at the time of its winter encampment from 1778 to 1779 at Redding, Connecticut. In 1779, when Old Put was sixty, he made a dramatic mounted escape from pursuing British dragoons, riding headlong down the perilous, one hundred steps carved in the precipice at Horse Neck, Greenwich. (See Walk 2, Putnam Memorial.)

Of all of Israel Putnam's flamboyant exploits, perhaps none is more familiar and renowned than his encounter with the she-wolf. For several years Putnam and his farm neighbors were losing stock to a marauding lone wolf; this wolf had a distinctive foot print due to the loss of its toes in a trap. When several of Putnam's sheep disappeared in one night, he vowed to get the wily killer, and enlisted the aid of five neighbors to hunt it in alternating pairs. Two members of the team constantly and relentlessly trailed the wolf, day after day, until finally they tracked her through the snow to her lair. They tried smoking her out of the stronghold without success. Next they sent in the hounds; but after being severely mauled, the dogs would not reenter the cave.

In desperation Putnam decided to squeeze through the long, low, narrow passageway himself to confront the beast with a birch-bark torch and trusty smooth-bore

TRAIL TIPS

Outhouses located in the state park, along with picnic areas and other trails. Wolf Den Drive is not paved; be alert for ruts and use caution if your car doesn't have good ground clearance. Wolf Den has an optional access from a nearby parking lot for those who wish to shorten the walk. Pick up a detailed trail map available at the ranger station, located just inside the park entrance. Pack in your trail refreshments or pick some up in Putnam.

gun. Tying a rope to his ankle, he crawled into the deep, dark dungeon, instructing his companions on the outside to drag him out fast if he yanked the rope twice. In the excitement their signals got crossed, and they hauled him out so fast his jacket and shirt were stripped off over his head; he lost part of his breeches and much of his hide. Removing the rope, he wryly stated that he'd rather face the wolf without friendly help. After being driven back once by the wolf, he returned later that same day, shot her, then dragged the heavy carcass out by the ears.

The Putnam Wolf Den is in the Mashamoquet Brook State Park in Pomfret township. To reach the den drive to the junction of Route 101 with Route U.S. 44 in Pomfret. Wolf Den Drive (a dirt-and-stone road that is not maintained in winter) is at the south side of this junction. Parking spots are abundant along the route, which, depending on road conditions and the ground clearance of your vehicle, may be impassable. Park and walk the road a short distance to the beginning of the red trail, which is a pleasant, fairly level walk through woodlands. At the terminus of the red trail (a map of the park is posted prominently at the juncture), head left a short distance to the stone Indian Chair (taking a right turn leads to the Wolf Den). The stone chair is a two-person-size natural formation perched atop slabs of smooth rock. It is a delightful spot to enjoy lunch while seated in the chair. After your break backtrack to the juncture (and map) and continue on the trail straight ahead to see the Wolf Den.

Pass through a swampy area filled with an abundance of ferns during warmer months; cross a wooden boardwalk, then up a hill past boulders. The low-lying area is a good place to spot salamanders and small critters who love the cool, damp area. In spring skunk cabbage, trillium, and Jack-in-the-pulpit may be seen sprouting through the rich dark muck, along with uncurling fronds of fiddlehead ferns.

The famous Wolf Den is a short uphill climb on a well-worn path with natural stone steps. Large, erratic, glacial boulders are scattered helter-skelter in the woods, seemingly thrown by an unseen giant's hand.

The den itself is a slot-like cave. Bring the past to life by telling the story of Putnam and imagine what it was like to finally track the she-wolf to her lair and enter the dark narrow den.

After a break continue on the trail to Table Rock, a naturally formed "table" large enough to picnic atop and a perfect stop for a trail snack. Head north again on the red trail to the road. At about 1.43 miles from the start of the walk is a stone well now clogged with debris and sticks—but of interest because of the tiny flat shelf located inside the lip and the rock platform that was used to retrieve a bucket or bring up food kept cool in the well.

As the trail meanders along, you soon reach Wolf Den Drive; from here it's a short walk back to your vehicle.

Should you have more time, there is an extensive network of trails in the park, including a short, easy loop nature trail.

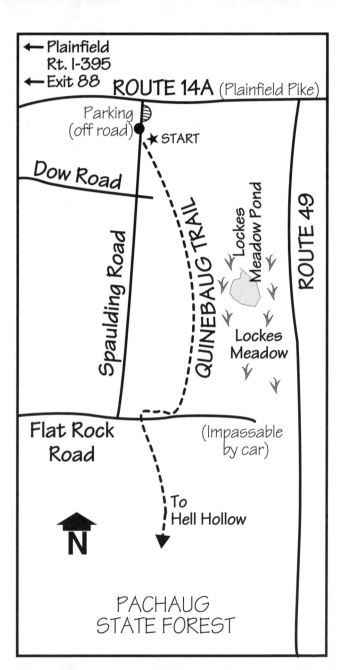

54

Lockes Meadow
Plainfield

A relaxing, nearly level-ground walk through woods to marshy meadows and to water. There are views of native wildflowers and pond inhabitants in a quiet setting. Suitable for all but use care near watery, mucky edges. The flowers are most abundant in the spring.

The Quinebaug Trail is part of the Connecticut Blue Trail System. It is 6.4 miles long and lies almost entirely within the Pachaug State Forest. The northern section of this trail is in the town of Plainfield; the southern portion is in Voluntown.

The northern terminus of the Quinebaug Trail is at the junction of Spaulding Road and Route 14A (Plainfield Pike). From the junction of Routes 14A and 49 in the town of Sterling, Spaulding Road is 1.9 miles west.

Turn south onto Spaulding Road from Route 14A and drive .4 mile to where the blue-blazed trail enters a woods road. Leave your car and proceed afoot, following the blazed trail, which is primarily a woodland trail. Lockes Meadow, a swampy wetland area near a pond, is about 1.5 miles from the starting point. Blazes in this area may be poor; bear right at the fork just before the pond. See pond—and then meadow—on your left. You can then retrace your steps to your car. (If you continue past the meadow, bear left at the next fork to reach dirt Flat Rock Road, 1.9 miles from the start.)

During seasons of normal rainfall the Lockes area appeals to a wide variety of birds and wildlife. The trail offers opportunities for picnicking, exploring, and nature study. Carry a camera and/or binoculars and a magnifying glass. Wear waterproofed footwear, or carry slip-on boots, should you desire to investigate the swampy area where many lovely flowers may be found.

Jack-in-the-pulpit is one of the most striking wild plants that can be found in springtime, alongside trillium (whose flowers and leaves have three leaves or petals), violets, and other lesser-known wildflowers. To find "Jack" carefully lift the dropping "leaf" that forms the hood of this plant and see the spathe, known as "Jack," standing in his pulpit. Use care not to damage the plant. The semi-rare moccasin flower, also called lady's slipper, can sometimes be seen in this area.

It is estimated that there are some 500-odd species of native and introduced wildflowers in the northeastern United States.

The *hepatica*, or liverleaf, prefers the leafmold soils of the high dry woodland, open woods, and forest slopes. The inconspicuous, fragile, single flowers, varying from lilac to bluish or white in color, defiantly push their way into the cold world while their hesitant leaves remain deeply hidden in their fuzzy wrappings, awaiting more favorable weather. The frail and delicate-appearing blossoms stand the stress and hardships that often shatter their robust and hardy-looking companions.

The name *hepatica* comes from the Greek word meaning liver. The flower in all probability was given the name because its leaf resembles the outline of a liver. As a consequence, the plant was used as a remedy for liver complaints, perhaps because omen-conscious people believed mother nature was indicating the use to which her creation might be applied.

Note: A southern section of the Quinebaug Trail is described in Walk 55. It is possible to walk south past the meadows to Devil's Den and Hell Hollow for a longer walk through woodlands and over interesting rock formations.

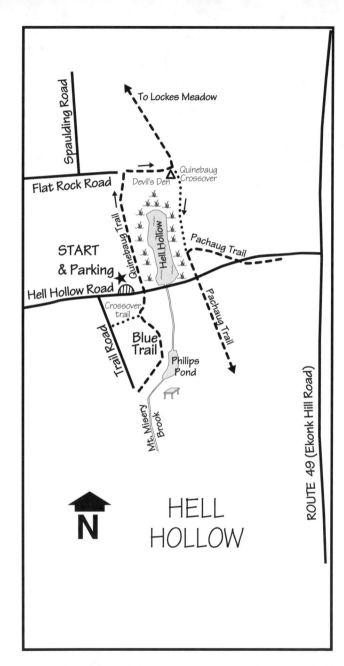

Spaulding Road

To Lockes Meadow

Flat Rock Road

Quinebaug Crossover

Devil's Den

Quinebaug Trail

Hell Hollow

Pachaug Trail

START & Parking

Hell Hollow Road

Crossover trail

Pachaug Trail

Trail Road

Blue Trail

Philips Pond

Mt. Misery Brook

N

HELL HOLLOW

ROUTE 49 (Ekonk Hill Road)

55

Hell Hollow
Plainfield

A walk through woods along well-worn paths that lead around a swampy pond, over an exposed rock road, and past numerous jumbles of boulders and mysterious crevices. Suitable for all if you choose a short section to explore—the entire circuit is more than 5 miles.

One of the easy and pleasant walks of the Connecticut Blue Trail System—despite its ominous topographical names: Hell Hollow, Devil's Den, and Misery Brook—is on the Quinebaug Trail.

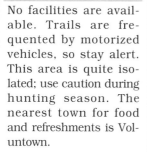

TRAIL TIPS

No facilities are available. Trails are frequented by motorized vehicles, so stay alert. This area is quite isolated; use caution during hunting season. The nearest town for food and refreshments is Voluntown.

The Quinebaug Trail is only 6.4 miles long; its southern section is in the town of Voluntown, its northern half in Plainfield. The Plainfield–Voluntown boundary is also the Windham–New London county line. The trail is mostly woods roads in the Pachaug State Forest.

To reach the Hell Hollow segment of the trail, take Route 14A to Route 49 south approximately 3 miles to Hell Hollow Road. Approaching from the south, in Voluntown and Routes 138 and 165, follow Route 49 north 5 miles to Hell Hollow Road.

Turn west onto Hell Hollow Road and follow it about 1.5 miles to where the Quinebaug Trail, indicated by blue blazes, crosses the road. A large pond and swampy area, through which Mount Misery Brook flows, is on the north side of the road, .1 mile before the trail. Park your car off the traveled portion of highway.

Head north on the sandy rock path into the woods on the blue-blazed trail, which follows a woods road all the way to Flat Rock Road, about 2.25 miles from your parked car. Flat Rock Road is well named—the smooth, road-sized exposed rock resembles a whale's back and the path follows it.

Turn right (east) onto Flat Rock Road and follow the blazed trail for approximately .75 mile to Devil's Den. The den is a mass of jumbled boulders and ledges just off the south shoulder of Flat Rock Road. This is an interesting area to explore. Springs flow out of the jumbled rock; stay alert for the possibility of snakes and other critters while exploring.

The trail between Hell Hollow Road and Flat Rock Road follows high ground; deep, sunken Hell Hollow is below to the east, and still east of the hollow is a predominant, high ridge. The woods road trail is an easy one to hike, and there are numerous ledges off the main path that invite inspection.

At about 3.5 miles from the start is a loop trail marked in yellow; it can be followed back to Hell Hollow Road for a total walk of about 5 miles. Be sure to periodically check for the blazes to ensure the correct path.

This route requires a short jaunt on Hell Hollow Road, past the pond, to the parking lot.

From your parking spot on Hell Hollow Road, you can also head west on Hell Hollow, then south on the

Quinebaug Trail or on Trail Road (dirt) for less than a mile to Philips Pond, a lovely spot with a waterfall and picnic area.

Note: Lockes Meadow, the northern section of the Quinebaug Trail, is described in Walk 54. It is possible to continue walking north on the Quinebaug Trail to the meadows and lengthen your walk to an all-day exploration.